GLORY REVEALED

david nasser

Printed in the United Sates of America

ISBN: 10: 0-9792479-1-8
ISBN: 13: 978-0-9792479-1-0

Cover Illustration: Nicholas Wilton
Jacket Design: Tim Parker
Inside Layout: LeAnn Gentry

To my parents

Khosrow Nasser

and

Simin Matini Nasser

to whom I will always be indebted.

DAVID WOULD LIKE TO THANK

The writing of this book has been a true team effort. I am extremely grateful to Adrienne Gray, Jessica Wolstenholm, LeAnn Gentry, Dana Davis, and Jennifer Nasser. Thank you ladies for spending countless hours on this project.

Jesus, you are glory revealed. I pray that this book will further your kingdom. Jennifer, Rudy, and Rebecca Grace for your unending support. You are beautiful. Our Nasser, Morgan, and Davis families, we love you. The Powells, for the truest kind of friendship. The talented team at Creative Trust, Word Distribution, Snap Republic, Tim Parker, and Nicholas Wilton for the art cover.

C O N T E N T S

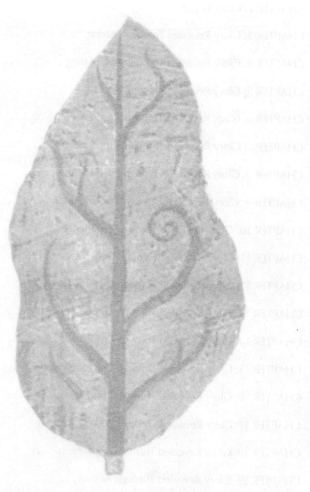

Everyone was crying but me. To the right of me was a lady with her hands held high and tears streaming down her face. To the left of me a man who was on his knees, wiping his eyes, and singing at the top of his lungs. I was standing between them, listening to the worship leader shout, "I want to touch you! I want to see your face! I want to know you more..." One by one, people were making their way down the aisle, flooding the altar. It felt as though God was revealing himself to everyone... everyone but me.

I was trapped. Whatever the congregation was sensing—I wasn't. I was wide-awake in a sea of people clearly receiving something divine. My heart desperately wanted to be right there with them, so what did I do? I closed my eyes, lifted my hands, and sang even louder, hoping not to get left behind.

I wanted to see what everyone else was seeing.
Touch what everyone else was touching.
Feel what everyone else was feeling.
Know what everyone else was getting to know.

Have you ever been there? Have you ever felt as though when it comes to connecting with God, you're missing out? Someone at Sunday school shares about "all that God has been saying to them lately." You hear statements like, "We saw God in a powerful way...," or "God spoke to me...," or "My walk with God..." It sounds like God is busy making the rounds and visiting everyone at your church, but somehow, you've landed on the black list. If you've ever felt that way, welcome to the club.

Throughout history, man has always longed to see the face of the invisible God. Because, as Christians, our faith affects us in an intimate and relational way, we try to apply human sensibilities to describe our relationship with the Lord. We use statements such as "walk and talk" or "hear and see" —all of which are physical descriptions. Even the psalmist used physical metaphors to express his yearning for God's presence.

"Taste and see that the Lord is good." (Ps. 34:8)

"I thirst for God, the living God. When can I come and appear before God?" (Ps. 42:2)

The truth is, none of us has ever seen the actual face of God with our own eyes or heard his voice with our ears, because God is a spirit and does not have a body like man. The problem isn't with our eyes or ears; it's with our souls. When we read the story of Moses interceding for the Israelites at Mt. Sinai, we are reminded that seeing the face of a holy God is something no sinful man can physically bear. God had to hide Moses in the crack of a mountain, and shield Moses's face with his hand as he passed by, revealing just a glimpse of his glory.

As a believer, one day in heaven I will see him face to face. The book of Revelation tells us in chapter 22, "They will see his face, and his name will be on their foreheads." That's really exciting and all, but what do I do until then? What about today while I am still here on earth?

How do I have a real life relationship with a God that cannot be seen? A God who is invisible? A God who I know is there? Sure, I've seen his creation—his endless majesty on a starry night. I can sense his infinite detail in the glory of a sunset. I feel his power in the rushing wind of a storm. I can look on a newborn baby and experience the miracle of God's tenderness. I see the evidence of his existence, but it's not enough. Everywhere I look I see his fingerprints, but I long to see his face.

How do I see God when I'm suffering from cancer or when my best friend betrays me? How can I hear him when I can't decide which job to take, or whom to marry? I need the Lord to communicate with me—to reveal himself.

INTRODUCTION

Is this a cruel joke God has decided to play? Some cosmic version of hide and seek where he creates in us a longing to see him but never allows us to find him? Hardly. The God of the universe has gone to great lengths to make himself known to us. We might not physically see his face or hear his voice, but we can always be assured that he is present. God is not hiding; he is actively revealing himself to us.

This book is about learning to see and to hear God in our everyday lives. God is not silent; we just have to learn **how** to listen. He is not absent; we just have to know **where** to look. Sometimes we say, "I want to see you," and God says, "I've been here all the while." We say, "I want to hear you," and he responds, "I never stopped talking." May God use this book to help you dig into the Word so that you can see, hear, and experience God in life changing ways.

God the Creator is so creative in the ways that he makes himself known. He shows himself through creation, circumstances, other people—everything. But in no place has he revealed himself more powerfully than through the Word: Jesus, the Word made flesh, and then through the Bible, the written Word.

Jesus, the Word made flesh, came to say that God does not want to be a mystery to you. Mankind has an incomplete view of who God is, and Jesus came to clear it up. Nowhere else can we see God more evidently than through Christ. The apostle John tells us that, "...the Word became flesh and dwelt among us, and we have seen his glory, glory as of the only Son from the Father, full of grace and truth." God the indescribable became describable when Jesus came down. Mankind got a glimpse of God with their eyes, and God made a way for us to have a relationship with him eternally. This is what we celebrate at Christmas. Not so much the birth of a baby named Jesus, but the incarnation of God into flesh. If we want to "see" God we can look to his Son.

The Bible, the written Word, is also used by God to clearly reveal to us who he is and how he wants our relationship with him to be. His Word speaks into our lives; convicting, comforting, clarifying, and calling us to live a life that brings honor and gives glory to him. If we want to "hear" God's voice, we hear it in the Scriptures.

In this book, we are going to focus on the revelation of God through his written Word. Throughout these twenty chapters we will look at places in Scripture where God reveals himself in different ways. Chapter after chapter, we will be reminded that God is alive and he's constantly speaking to us through his Word. There really is no adequate way to describe what a treasure we have been given in the Holy Scriptures. It's an infallible work given directly to us by a God who wants us to understand his relationship with us. He could have just left us in the dark, guessing at his agenda, but he didn't.

If you're going through a tough time, we will look at how God is actively involving himself with you as we study the Biblical character Job.

If things are going really well for you, we'll discover how God walks with you on your mountaintops by looking at the story of Moses.

Maybe you have a friend who is living in darkness and sin. We'll see how God can speak into the situation as we look at the relationship between King David and the prophet Nathan.

As we study God's Word in these twenty different chapters, my prayer is that you will sense one common thread: God is present and revealing himself powerfully through his Holy Scriptures. We must come to a place where we're feeding our hunger to know God with the meat of the Word and stop continuously stuffing our spiritual bellies full of events and emotional encounters.

How sweet Your word is to my taste—[sweeter] than honey to my mouth. (Ps. 119:103)

You've heard the phrase *carpe diem*—seize the day. Here is another charge: *Carpe liber*—seize the book!

When my son Rudy first came to live with us at the age of seven, I loved to watch him eat. Orphaned in Guatemala, he had such a different hunger than what we're used to seeing here in the United States. To him, a meal was such a treasure.

His eyes would open wide as saucers when a roasted chicken was brought to the table. He would slowly savor every bite leaving absolutely no meat on the bones. Sometimes he would even break the bones apart and suck the marrow, enjoying all of it. He wasn't afraid to seize the chicken!

Now after living here for a while, used to having bigger portions and constant access to an overstuffed fridge, he's pickier. There's nothing wrong with being so well taken care of, it's just that sometimes in a blessed society we don't get to appreciate the nuances of what's placed in front of us. Overwhelmed with so many options to help us study the Word of God, we end up nibbling here and there, never really digging in for a full meal. Most of us start way too many devotional books, only to set them aside, distracted by other choices. There are hundreds of good free devotionals on the Web, sermon series, Bible studies every night of the week, and so much more. It's like an all-you-can-eat buffet—there are so many choices that we've almost become too full to really savor the truth. Our blessings have become something of a hindrance.

The challenge is to approach this book, and any book with redemptive value, with spiritual hunger. Slowly read through it, savoring every truth on every page. Don't just microwave it—let it slow cook in your spirit. Rather than reading from beginning to end in a couple of sittings, I'd like to encourage you to read a chapter every day, using it as you would a devotional.

Underline words or phrases that speak to you. Write in the margins questions about things that you want to revisit. Better yet, challenge my thinking—go back to the source in Scripture and ask God to show you what he wants revealed to you.

But let this book be nothing more than a beginning. Let it be something that whets your appetite for Scripture, giving you a hunger to get all of the meat off of the bones as you search for more and more revelation. This book should ultimately call you to dive into THE book: The Bible.

So before we get started, let me pray for you.

Great God, use these next twenty chapters. Allow them to be twenty different windows to see who You are. But let them also be twenty windows we open up for you to enter into us.

We pray that you would bring great revelation through these pages and use them in our lives so they won't just be information, but in-me-formation.

In the name of King Jesus, Amen.

The LORD your God is among you,
a warrior who saves.
He will rejoice over you with gladness.
He will bring [you] quietness with His love.
He will delight in you with shouts of joy.
(Zephaniah 3:17)

Glory Revealed Through Quieting Love

If you're looking to find history and art that moves the soul toward the glory of God, Rome is the perfect place to start. From the works of Michelangelo in the Sistine Chapel to the history of thousands of Christians martyred at the Colosseum, you just see glory—God's glory brightly revealed everywhere you look. Even in the most unexpected places.

A few years ago, I found myself alone, wandering the cobblestone streets of Rome. I was in the middle of a sabbatical season, traveling in search of reflection and inspiration. After a few days there I found my rhythm. I would wake up at noon, spend time in prayer, and get ready to head out for the day. I would visit one, maybe two places for reflection—not rushing, but sipping slowly what God was rationing out to me. I didn't want to miss the message behind the art.

This routine would take me late into the night when, around 10:00 pm, I'd end up at a patio restaurant. I'd dine alone and revisit the day's journey over an authentic bowl of pasta. By the way, this is typical in Rome. The Italians eat lunch around 3:00 pm and have dinner at 10:00 pm. When in Rome... right?

One night I found myself in a little trattoria just outside the Vatican. The large patio was well lit with candlelight, and the people were loud and boisterous. It was everything you would imagine an outdoor Italian restaurant to be.

As I sat there, I noticed a big Italian family starting to gather for some sort of reunion. As all of the family members began arriving—the father and mother, the children, the grandparents—it was only fair to say that this family was not quiet. Every time another member of the family arrived, you could hear the welcoming cheers. Grandma was yelling and gesturing about whom should sit where, while the rest of the family went around greeting with kisses and giant embraces.

Even though I don't speak Italian, it was obvious who was who in this dramatic and verbose family just by watching their body language. At the center of the table, equally confident in calling the waiters to attention as weighing in on all the conversations, was the family patriarch. And seated next to him, a wide-eyed princess with curly hair—his little daughter, no more than eight or nine years old. She reminded me a bit of my daughter, Grace.

I sat at the table across from them, reading and watching, when the local flower peddler entered the scene. You know the guy—the one from the touristy street corner or romantic restaurant. The guy with the huge painter's bucket filled with long-stemmed roses who, right in front of your date, tries to guilt you into buying one? Well, his cousin is alive and well in Rome, and he found my table. I guess he assumed my date had gone to the bathroom while my nose was buried in the Bible. I politely declined his pitch, and watched him as he moved onto the family gathering.

Just as I suspected, our family patriarch would have none of the peddler's antics. With the crinkle of his brow and the flick of his wrist, he sent the street peddler on his way, barely skipping a beat of conversation. But then something happened that changed everything. The father caught a glimpse of his daughter's eyes, engaged by the sight of the roses.

He stopped talking to the grandfather and kept looking at his daughter, whose eyes were fixed on the roses. He jumped from his chair and ran to catch up with the peddler. He whispered something in the peddler's ear, exchanged nods, and with one sweeping movement, grabbed every rose from the bucket and thrust them into his daughter's arms.

I don't know if you've ever seen a little girl holding nearly one hundred long-stemmed roses—I certainly hadn't before this moment—but it's a sight that will suck the wind out of an entire room. Everyone in the restaurant fell silent as the loudest and most expressive guy there left us all speechless. Even those who didn't see the amazing gesture of love were sucked in by the gaze of all of us who had just witnessed the amazing act. That father quieted us all with his love.

This is no ordinary love the prophet is referring to.

The little girl was absolutely stunned. The peddler offered his bucket, but she refused to let go of the giant pile of roses she could barely wrap her arms around. Instead, she sat there quietly through dinner, intermittently staring down at the roses and up at her dad. She didn't need words to thank him, they would have just fallen short—she was speechless with awe.

That father lavished his little girl with his love. He wasn't the least bit interested in those roses until he saw her face. The moment he realized what those roses would mean to her, he didn't hesitate. He wasn't afraid to make a mess when the roses were dripping water from the bucket. He didn't haggle with the peddler over the price or wait until the next day to get a better deal at Costco. He refused to lose the moment.

That's what the grace of God is—an enormous bundle of roses. More than you can wrap your arms around. Given in a moment so right that it floors you. A moment so right that you're left speechless.

Have you ever gone to Niagara Falls and found yourself covered in the mist, thunderstruck? Did you catch your first glimpse of the Grand Canyon and find yourself with absolutely nothing to say? Have you ever seen a groom, after watching his bride walk down the aisle, be so caught up in the moment that all he could do is choke through his vows?

There are moments in life when it's better to resign your lips as you think, *I'm not even going to try.* This must have been the kind of magnificent love the prophet Zephaniah was referring to.

The LORD your God is among you,
a warrior who saves.
He will rejoice over you with gladness.

He will bring [you] quietness with His love.
He will delight in you with shouts of joy. (Zeph. 3:17)

This is no ordinary love the prophet is referring to. It's mighty. It's more roses than you can wrap your arms around. A deeper canyon than any you've ever seen. Beyond your wildest dreams, it rushes in like Niagara Falls. God lavishes us with so much more than we could ever deserve.

He wants us smitten.
Dumfounded. Flat-out taken.

But why does he do it? Because his glory is revealed when he shows us a love so mighty, powerful, and pure that we find ourselves wanting him even more. He wants us smitten. Dumfounded. Flat-out taken.

There was one image that night in Italy that left a searing impression on me. It wasn't the roses or even the little girl that blew me away. It was the amazing love of the father. He took great delight in the act, and the little girl just went along for the ride. It made me want to introduce myself and shake his hand. I would have liked to have gotten to know the man who had the ability to quiet an entire restaurant with one undeniably generous act.

Thinking back to the little girl, I'm certain that act will sear itself in her memory as well. She'll be affected by it for years to come. Once you've been given that kind of love, you'll never accept any less. Can you imagine that little girl growing up to marry some selfish loser? No! She'll be immune to a man like that. Her daddy raised the standard for her forever.

God does the same for us so he can forever win our hearts and steal our affection! He's constantly looking for ways to suck the air out of the room so that we have no choice but to recognize his glory. But sometimes, just like in any relationship, we begin to take his love for granted. Instead of being quieted by his all encompassing love, we whine.

Look around you. You have more than one book to read. More than just a slice of bread to eat. More than one shirt to wear. Do you ever lose sight of how many blessings touch your life? Do you ever let yourself come to expect it? Is it time to reflect upon just how much he's done for you?

How does he love you? Let me count the ways.

LORD, Your faithful love [reaches] to heaven Your faithfulness to the skies. (Ps. 36:5)

But God proves His own love for us in that while we were still sinners Christ died for us! (Rom. 5:8)

...nor height, nor depth, nor any other created thing will have the power to separate us from the love of God that is in Christ Jesus our Lord! (Rom. 8:39)

Love consists in this: not that we loved God, but that He loved us and sent His Son to be the propitiation for our sins. (1 John 4:10)

For God loved the world in this way: He gave His One and Only Son, so that everyone who believes in Him will not perish but have eternal life. (John 3:16)

God loves us so lavishly, that in addition to the ways he pours out his love on our lives now, he left us a trail of love letters through his infallible Word. He created a masterpiece that speaks to us from history even as he speaks to us through blessings and grace in our every day lives. Talk about leaving us speechless!

I went to Rome in search of revelation through art, and I left with an understanding so much more profound than what I was looking for. Sitting there in that piazza, reflecting on everything that happened, it became clear to me—I am the little girl in this story. I'm a constant target of the glory of God—a love revealed at any expense.

Additional scriptures for personal study:

Exodus 20:6   Romans 8:28-29

1 John 4:16

How is God's glory revealed through his quieting love?

Think of the times in your life when God has sucked the air out of the room on your behalf. Describe those moments when he quieted you with his love.

Take stock of all of the blessings in your life. Have you taken his love for granted? List the things, apparent and not apparent, that display his love for you.

JOURNAL

USE THIS PAGE TO JOURNAL ABOUT WHAT GOD IS REVEALING TO YOU TODAY.

The LORD your God is among you,
a warrior who saves.
He will rejoice over you with gladness.
He will bring [you] quietness with His love.
He will delight in you with shouts of joy.
(Zephaniah 3:17)

Glory Revealed Through Conversation

This is one of those moments when, for the sake of illustration, I have to confess something that I am not proud of at all. As you read this, know that I have repented, and looking back, I can't believe I actually did what I did. But now that I've got your attention...

A few years ago, I was speaking at a weeklong conference. This particular event had a hospitality room for me and the worship team to hang out and eat dinner in between sessions. The room was great and so was the food, but there was one problem. Like most Christian events, there were volunteer staffers assigned to help out in the backstage area. The problem was the staffer in charge of hospitality. To say that his definition of the role of hospitality staff was different than mine was an understatement.

My first memory of my new friend was that of his face inches from mine as he told me that he had read both of my books and was excited for us to finally meet. Personal space aside, that was encouraging and I really appreciated it. But things went downhill from there.

Every time the worship team and I would sit down to eat or try to unwind before the next session, there he was, involved in every single conversation. The leadership team and I would meet backstage to talk about the night's schedule, and he'd chime in, involving himself in the planning. On the last night, one of the musicians asked me if I wanted to go out afterward for some coffee and hang time. Our staffer buddy piped in to ask, "Where are we going? I know a great place!" The guy had no boundaries. He wanted to be included so badly that he didn't realize what kind of personal space was appropriate. As long as he was around, there would be no privacy.

This might be way too honest, but frankly, he bothered me. He was relentless to the point that I found myself hesitating to go into the hospitality room in fear that I would run into him. If you're reading this and you're thinking that I'm a total jerk for feeling that way, then you might want to go ahead and burn this book before you read any further—it only gets worse from here.

On the last morning, he approached me with a smile, telling me that it was such a blessing to get to know the real me. How I wasn't just a minister on stage, but backstage as well. "I feel as though we have really connected as I hoped we would," he said. And then came the moment I will forever regret. He asked for my cell phone number.

"Why don't you give me your cell number and when the summer is over, I'll call you and we can hang out!"

Do you know what I did? I gave him my number. Well, almost. I gave him my cell phone number, with one wrong digit. On purpose! That way when he called, he'd get a wrong number, and if I ever saw him again, he couldn't get mad. He might even think he accidentally pushed the wrong number as he was storing it.

As he walked away, I was actually proud of my quick thinking.

An hour later conviction set in. What kind of minister was I? I tried to tell myself that he was a genuine nuisance and that he was in the wrong to ask for something so personal as my cell phone number in the first place. But no matter how much I tried to reason my way out of it, I had lied and I was deeply disappointed in myself.

I had other options. I could have asked him to email me instead, or even used the moment to speak some brotherly advice into his life. What if I had said, "You know, I'm not ready to give my personal number out to you yet." Then maybe I could have encouraged him and gracefully given him advice about not being so overbearing. But rather than investing in him and having a conversation, I just lied.

I had gotten too big for my own britches. Guys like this fellow are the very people I was called to befriend and minister to. He was lonely, looking for conversation and relationship. Sure he was a pest, but when it comes down to it, we all are. That weekend I actually traded my cell number with several others, possibly even in front of him. They were those who I wanted to get to know better. People I wanted to have further conversation with. I just didn't want to give access to this guy. He bothered me, so I didn't want to bother with him.

Aren't you glad that God doesn't treat us the way I treated that volunteer? Aren't you glad God isn't like me? Like us? Before you judge what I did that day, and I am the first to confess what I did was wrong, ask yourself if you would do the same—if you see some people as worthy of your time and some not.

Have you ever looked at the caller ID on your phone and decided to let it go straight to voicemail because you didn't want to have a conversation with the one calling? You might have thought, *It's only so and so. I can't believe they're calling me again. When are they going to get a clue?!* Then just a minute later you received a call from a person that you've left numerous messages for and you answered excitedly without hesitation! We all do it—we categorize and determine who is worthy of conversation and who is not.

Life is about relationship; it's about conversation.

Aren't you glad that the God of the universe has given us access to himself? When we call upon the name of the Lord, whether in prayer or worship, he answers every time. He doesn't think, *Oh, it's the President. He's important so I better get that,* and then see my call and think, *Oh it's that persistent pest David Nasser again. He always wants to talk.* God doesn't categorize us and let us go to voicemail when he's too busy. How awful would it be if the Lord thought, *This person is way too needy. I wish I hadn't given him access in the first place.*

Jeremiah 33:2-3 promises us that God is not nearly as petty as we are:

> **The LORD who made the earth, the LORD who forms it to establish it, the LORD is His name, says this: Call to Me and I will answer you and tell you great and wondrous things you do not know.**

There is great value in knowing that God desires conversation with us and that our relationship with him is not a monologue where we leave messages in hope that we're worthy of a call back. It is intimate conversation that makes any relationship worthwhile. Rather than sitting there watching God do his thing, or God from afar watching us do ours, we engage in a relationship filled with spiritual dialogue.

Life is about relationship; it's about conversation. A dialogue—not a monologue. It's a symphony of hearing and being heard in return, of loving and being loved. We learn and grow from each other. We support and serve each other. And if we model our relationships after God's, we find so much joy in each other that we rejoice and sing.

There are few things in this world as hurtful as realizing you're in a one-way relationship. When you pour energy, hope, and love into someone—placing your heart in their hands—only to hear nothing back, it's one of the loneliest feelings I can think of.

I venture to say that we've all had the kind of friend who calls to tell us the details of her joys, hurts, and experiences only to find an excuse to jump off of the phone the moment we begin to talk about our life. How about the family member who claims he loves us but does absolutely nothing to make us feel welcome or comfortable? The friend that breaks off our plans as soon as she gets a better offer, or worse, doesn't show at all.

...every song we sing to the Lord is a duet and not a solo.

One of the most marvelous things about our relationship with God is that it truly is a dialogue. We aren't just here on earth, worshipping a Creator who simply soaks up our love. Rather, he's so involved in our affection that he's actually in the midst of it.

Zephaniah 3:17 says:

The LORD your God is among you,
a warrior who saves.
He will rejoice over you with gladness.
He will bring [you] quietness with His love.
He will delight in you with shouts of joy.

I love that he sings over us. We put so much emphasis on singing worship songs to God, that it's so reassuring to read in Scripture that he sings back.

We sing, "I love you, Lord." He may sing, "I love you, child."

We sing, "You're all I want." He may sing, "I want all of you."

We sing, "I want to know you more." He may sing, "I know everything about you and I want you to know me more."

It's a sobering reality that every song that we sing to the Lord is a duet and not a solo. In singing, we are responding to him, and in real time he is responding to us.

If you're wondering who started the song to begin with, it was him. Worship is our response to God. He is actually the initiator. Long before we were born, the great conductor began his symphony of glory. Psalm 139:16 reads, "Your eyes saw me when I was formless; all [my] days were written in Your book and planned before a single one of them began."

Sometimes I wonder if his songs to us are like a lullaby—songs that he's been impressing on our soul since our creation. Tender melodies that allow us to recognize his voice and his presence in every situation. Songs that come alive in our spirit through a sunrise or a rainstorm, or even in a worship song.

New mothers sing to their babies even before they are born. In the days of waiting, they sit in their rocking chairs rubbing their bellies, overflowing with love and expectation. All their hopes and prayers are wrapped into a language of tender lullabies they sing to their unborn little ones. Mothers know it will be a while yet before their babies can understand the words, or understand even a fraction of the love they feel, but it's a blessing they know in their hearts won't be lost on the child who can hear even in the womb.

When my wife, Jennifer, was pregnant with our daughter Grace, she sang these words from a classic hymn: "Grace, grace, God's grace, grace that will pardon and cleanse within, grace that is greater than all our sin."

She continued to sing it to Grace as a tiny infant. She sang it to her as an adventurous toddler. She sang it to her in her terrible twos. Even now, as a child, Jennifer can sing that song to our daughter to calm her when her emotions or her energies get too high. Sometimes now Jennifer will sing to Grace when she's in distress, or if she's about to get a shot at the doctor's office. Grace immediately comes to a place of recognition and trust, familiarity and rest. She knows Jennifer's voice almost as if it left an imprint on our daughter's spirit. When she hears her mommy's voice, she's immediately brought back to a place of love and safety.

I wonder if the same is true for the songs that God sings over us. I'm certain my spirit knows them just like my daughter knows my wife's voice. But the words or the melody aren't exactly the point—Jennifer could have sung a Led Zeppelin song to Grace and it would have had the same effect because of the familiarity of her voice and the love in her tone. It won't be until Grace is more mature that she will come to an understanding of the amazing words of her own tender lullaby. I think it's God's way of letting me know he's my Father, singing over his child, bringing me to a place of love and safety. He's letting me know that he's mighty yet still tender enough to flow over me with song.

I think God sings over us whether we participate or not. But how much greater is it when we complete the conversation? When we sing back to him with our voices. When we sing back to him with our lives or when we symbolically hold our empty hands to him, letting him know that we can't make it without him. When we fill our hands with the tools needed to serve him. All the while, we know that he's singing over us.

We need to stop and listen to God's part of the conversation. We should let him quiet us with his love as he sings over us. We've got to stop being so loud and just listen to our Father. Let him tell us how much he loves us. Let him give us direction and purpose. Let him talk about what his plans are for us or what he wants us to do.

Just as he lets us pray to him, sing to him, and worship him, we need to stop and take the time to let him dwell in our midst, rejoice over us, and sing over us. To let him tenderly bring us back to a place where we trust him and know that he has us in his protection. A lot of times we don't understand the specifics of what he's singing, or what he's bringing us through. But we know by his tone that we're safe in the cradle of his arms.

Other times, I think a conversation is just what's needed.

He might sing to you through Scripture. He may show you a new truth in the Christmas story in the month of June. You may sing back, "O come let us adore him."

He may sing over you through the love of your family as you're sitting at the Thanksgiving table. You can pause and reflect and let your heart sing, "Praise God from whom all blessings flow."

He may sing over you with wisdom in a tricky situation. You can sing back with your obedience.

In your darkest hour, you may cry out to him by singing, "Help me just set aside the cares of this world and fall in love with you again." He may sing back by sending his Holy Spirit to comfort you.

You may wake up to the sound of the wind moving through the trees and sing, "How great is our God." He may sing back by renewing your strength.

It's a conversation that's never ending. It'll continue through all eternity. How many relationships can you say that about?

Whether God sings over us through a lullaby, revelation through Scripture, his faithfulness, his creation, or even a finite song, we may never know. But the fact is that he is engaging in a real conversation with his children. The God who is mighty to save us loves us so much that he's serenading our affection. He has gladly given you access—call him, sing to him, talk to him; he wants to reveal himself to you.

Additional scriptures for personal study:

Psalm 42:8   Ephesians 1:4

How is God's glory revealed through conversation?

God gave us the equivalent of an all-access, backstage pass to his throne. Do you spend as much time as you should be taking advantage of that great privilege? How can you spend more time with him in conversation?

Where are the places in your life where you can feel God singing over you? Are there places where you hear his voice louder than others? Is it at the edge of the ocean? Is it when you see a baby smile? Is it when he shows his provision?

USE THIS PAGE TO JOURNAL ABOUT WHAT GOD IS REVEALING TO YOU TODAY.

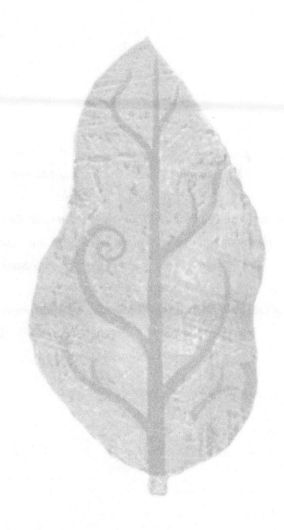

They sang the song of God's servant Moses,
and the song of the Lamb:
Great and awe-inspiring are Your works, Lord God, the Almighty;
righteous and true are Your ways, King of the Nations.
Lord, who will not fear and glorify Your name?
Because You alone are holy,
because all the nations will come and worship before You,
because Your righteous acts have been revealed.
(Revelation 15:3-4)

Glory Revealed Through Fearing

"Soldier." It's a title that must be earned. Earned by rushing off of a bus into a great unknown called "boot camp." Earned by having your head shaved and your clothing replaced by a nondescript uniform. Earned by having your will and your pride broken and fed to you by a man or woman known only as "drill sergeant."

Drill sergeants work for months on end, at the cost of their vocal chords, to break a recruit's reliance on his own identity. They spend exhaustive hours step-by-step alongside recruits in pre-dawn drills, late-night inspections, and rigorous physical training, so that through firm and repeat intimidation a mere man or woman is conditioned to become part of something greater.

They prepare the recruit to earn the title "soldier" in the United States Armed Forces. But recruits don't leave boot camp skilled in battle, able to fight anywhere in the world—they go to other camps for that. Sure, they'll leave boot camp with a basic understanding of how to put together a gun and what to do should they see the flash just before a mushroom cloud, but anyone can learn those things with a quick Google search. The entire purpose of boot camp is to give soldiers an attitude adjustment, a fear and awe of the man above them, and the man above that man, a blind trust in something much greater than themselves. That's what earns them the title "soldier."

A drill sergeant knows that if he doesn't instill a fear of authority in each recruit, they will be a danger to themselves and all around them in battle. A soldier has to have a greater fear of his commander's voice than his surroundings when bullets and bombs are flying. Otherwise, he and his unit won't have a chance to survive.

It's a great parallel to begin understanding how we should fear God. We give him obedience and trust, resigning our will to his will. We learn to fear his voice so that he can protect us and work his purposes in our lives. And we adjust our hearts to be in tune with his greater plans.

Fear and friendship are not enemies.

But there's a little more to it than just blind submission. Fearing God is a part of our relationship with him that unfolds in beautiful layers. One of the greatest examples of this I've ever heard is from Jerry Bridges' book *The Joy of Fearing God*. Jerry weaves a tale of how a young recruit makes it through boot camp to find out he's assigned to be the General's driver. The soldier has a fear of the General—a healthy fear mixed with respect, loyalty, and a little bit of awe. But even as their relationship grows and the soldier becomes more comfortable in their day-to-day interaction, the young soldier always addresses him with "Yes, sir" and "No, sir."

Duty calls, and their platoon is assigned to the battlefield. Though not on the frontlines, the General and his driver navigate hostile territory with regularity. One fateful day, their jeep strikes a land mine, seriously wounding both men. The General, despite his injuries, risks his life to pull the unconscious young soldier from the fiery wreckage.

In the months following the accident, the General recovers much more quickly than the young soldier, but he stops in daily to check up on him. It's here, baffled that such a powerful man would show him so much care, that the soldier's "fear" of the General becomes complete. He recognizes that the General loves him and would give his own life for him. Adding to the fear, respect, loyalty, and awe, the soldier now holds a deep love for the General.

Fear and friendship are not enemies. They are like the unlikely couple you see at the mall holding hands, strangely bound by love. God wants us to fear him so that he can work on our behalf, simultaneously building his relationship with us.

Fear of God is not the skewed fear that paints God as a tyrant out to crush us. Rather, it's a healthy fear of him that we begin to understand through Scripture. A fear fueled by awe and reverence. He could crush us—but that's not his plan. He wants to work all things together for the good of those who love him. But he still wants us to obey his command and know his voice so that we can be true soldiers in building his kingdom.

As we discover his plans to lovingly place us in the center of his will, it's important to remember that familiarity with God's love does not give us license to lose our reverence for him. That's because honor, obedience, and reverence are necessary to be intimate with him. We fear God because he holds the universe in his hands. When we submit our lives to him, the God of the universe takes our fear and returns it with love by delivering us personally! But after we receive his love, we can't ever lose the fear and respect of who he is.

People in this generation, in an attempt to be intimate with God, have teetered on the edge of losing respect and reverence for him. They confuse the great gift of his grace and mercy as a hall pass to disregard his voice on matters that aren't so warm and fuzzy. What they're missing is a healthy fear—obeying his commandments and submitting to his voice—that will actually bring them closer to him.

Fear is not a wall that separates us from God. It's an open door that gives us access to his love and protection. For reasons that elude every new parent, things like electric sockets are fascinating to an infant. When Grace was a baby, Jennifer and I had to set strong boundaries to protect her. Thankfully, at first all it took to keep her from harm was a little plastic shield. But as she grew older and could remove the socket protector, we had to become stern in our warnings. The discipline would always break her tender heart—and mine. But what hurts more? The sting of my cautionary voice, or the sizzle of a fork on tender skin when jammed into a wall socket? If my baby girl hadn't had a healthy fear of my voice, I couldn't protect her from danger she couldn't understand.

If we had been all hugs and smiles with Grace, there's a good chance she wouldn't have made it to pre-school alive. Even if she miraculously avoided harm, how would she know how to avoid it when Jennifer or I weren't around? We needed our baby girl to look up at us with big giant eyes in awe of our every move. We needed her to know the discipline of our hand and to fear it. And we needed her to trust that our discipline was for her own good.

God wants us to look up at him with big giant eyes in awe of his every move. He wants us to know the discipline of his hand and his voice and to fear it. He wants us to trust that his discipline is for our own good. He wants us to obey him so that our relationship can grow in love. And he wants us to fear him so that his glory can be revealed.

In Philippians 2:12, Paul extends these words:

So then, my dear friends, just as you have always obeyed, not only in my presence, but now even more in my absence, work out your own salvation with fear and trembling.

Ask Grace if we love her, and I know my little girl will tell you there aren't two people on this earth who love her more. Ask any soldier if his commanding officer has his best interest in mind, and he will go on and on about being part of a brotherhood unmatched. Ask anyone who is working out his salvation with fear and trembling, and you'll find someone who knows that God loves him more than he could have ever imagined.

So go ahead. Be of good fear.

Additional scriptures for personal study:

Psalm 96:9	Proverbs 1:7; 9:10
1 John 2:5-6	

How is God's glory revealed through fearing?

Why is it necessary to fear God? Why can't your relationship with him be all mercy and tenderness?

What would a life lacking the fear of God look like? Describe examples either from the world around you or from your own life.

USE THIS PAGE TO JOURNAL ABOUT WHAT GOD IS REVEALING TO YOU TODAY.

J O U R N A L

USE THIS PAGE TO JOURNAL ABOUT WHAT GOD IS REVEALING TO YOU TODAY.

I sought the LORD, and He answered me
and delivered me from all my fears.
Those who look to Him are radiant with joy;
their faces will never be ashamed.

(Psalm 34:4-5)

Glory Revealed Through Not Fearing

The sixth grade. It's a time when many boys become men. It's more than the beginning of puberty; it's the end of elementary school.

For me, the sixth grade was a horrifying time. In those days, I was a wedgy waiting to happen. My memories of sixth grade are memories of fear—of one guy. His name was Corbett.

I spent many days avoiding or running from Corbett. But here's the weirdest part—Corbett wasn't the bully at our school. He was a wimp just like me. I guess I was the one guy below him on the food chain, and the punishment rolled downhill.

Every day a band of bullies would gang up on Corbett, starting the cycle of pain. First they would mess with him, and then he would turn and mess with me. Corbett was their punching bag, and I was his.

I tried everything—reasoning with him, hiding from him, giving him my lunch, even bribing him. But nothing seemed to help. The truth is that hurt people... well, they hurt other people. Corbett had decided to deal with his hurt by delivering doses of pain to me.

Let me be clear here and say that I'm talking about pushes and shoves, not knives and guns. But when you're a kid, it's still scary. It's enough to give a sixth grader a perpetual complex. Finally one morning before school, I woke up with fear and dread of another day's events gurgling in my gut. I was so tired of the merry-go-round of pain that I went to my dad. It was a huge step for me.

Even though my dad is a loving man, he is also a proud military man. For me to admit to him that I couldn't handle myself was a risky proposition. What if I let him down? What if this showed him that I wasn't strong enough or brave enough to earn his respect? What if he couldn't trust me anymore? I knew I needed his help, but I was actually so fearful of my father's greatness, that I shut off my access to the assistance that would get me out of this never-ending cycle of fear.

What I was missing was this: My dad wanted the very best for me. He knew much better than I how to help me overcome my weaknesses, yet I was repeating my mistakes over and over again. All I had to do was reach out and ask for his help.

After listening quietly while I told him what waited for me at school every day, my dad replied simply, "Today after school, I will meet this Corbett." I was thrilled! The whole day I had visions of my strapping commando of a father punching out a sixth grader. This was going to be great! All I had to do was avoid Corbett until the final bell.

At three o'clock, I didn't waste a second in dashing toward the parking lot. I spotted my father's car and nearly jumped through the window. I could almost taste the safety inside. Except my father had a different plan.

"Son, stand out there and wait for Corbett. When he comes, you say to him 'Corbett, I don't want you to mess with me anymore.'"

"But Dad!" I argued.

"Son, stand there and wait for him."

I had no choice. My father had spoken. He was commanding me to stand up and face my fears. And as much as I feared the wrath of Corbett, the fear of what would happen if I disobeyed my father was much greater. Had anyone else given me those orders, I would have cut and run. Instead, I stood there in that parking lot, waiting for Corbett to finish taking his abuse for the day, knowing I was next.

After a few minutes of getting razed himself, a disheveled Corbett approached, looking to displace his latest misery on me. Even though I knew my father's eye was on me, I was still shaking ever so slightly.

"C-C-Corbett," I managed. "I'm tired of running from you. I don't w-want you to m-mess with me anymore."

"What did you say?" he demanded.

"Corbett," I replied, this time suddenly feeling my father's authority. "I don't want you to mess with me anymore."

Corbett's eyes grew wide as saucers. I thought it was because I had uttered some magic macho words my father handed down. But without my knowledge, rising in tandem with the words of a sixth grader shaking in his boots, an ex-Iranian military commander rose silently out of the car and stood behind me. As he did, the words of my mouth came alive to my attacker. I didn't need my father's strong arm—his very presence was more than enough.

What we shared was shelter in the shadow of my father.

In that moment—the moment that I stood up to Corbett—I had power because the fear of my father gave me courage to stand in the face of my tormentor. There I stood in the shadow of my father, sheltered and fearless. Corbett might have been bigger than me, but he was not bigger than my dad.

My father then took Corbett by the shoulder and walked him over to the school bullies who had roughed him up earlier. I didn't hear what he said on Corbett's behalf, but I can tell you that Corbett was never harassed again.

And Corbett never messed with me again.

I'd love to tell you that Corbett and I became friends that day, but we didn't. What I can tell you is that we were no longer enemies. What we shared was shelter in the shadow of my father. Mark Twain was once quoted as saying, "Courage is not absence of fear; it is control of fear, mastery of fear." My father never told me to stop fearing Corbett that day, he taught me to trust him in the midst of my fear. My fear of Corbett was a valid one. My dad never discounted my fear—he helped me face it and conquer it.

On my own, conquering my fear was not possible. With my dad, the impossible became reality. It's what Paul meant when he said, "I am able to do all things through Him who strengthens me" (Phil. 4:13). We can take our healthy fear of the Lord and use it to face our fears of this world.

Did you know that there are so many different kinds of fears out there that they each have a specific name? Here are a few of my favorites:

Arachnophobia—the fear of spiders
Acrophobia—the fear of heights
Agoraphobia—fear of open spaces or of being in crowded,
    public places
Anglophobia—fear of England or English culture
Anablophobia—fear of looking up
Catoptrophobia—fear of mirrors
Clinophobia—fear of going to bed
Coulrophobia—fear of clowns
Ereuthrophobia—fear of blushing
Gerontophobia—fear of old people
Homilophobia—fear of sermons
Kathisophobia—fear of sitting down
Leukophobia—fear of the color white
Lutraphobia—fear of otters
Rhytiphobia—fear of getting wrinkles
Stygiophobia—fear of hell
Zemmiphobia—fear of the great mole rat

It's amazing to me that some of these have merited names—how many times in life have you been threatened by an otter? No matter how silly they sound, these fears are all valid to someone. The easiest way to conquer them isn't to discount them; it's to upgrade your faith.

When we face our fears with faith in the Lord, God's strength is revealed. And his strength brings him glory. The more strength, the more glory.

When we trust and obey God's ways—his word, his voice—we can face the things that come against us. By putting our hope into something bigger than everything around us, our energy isn't wasted on fearing the little things. Instead, our Father actually teaches us how to handle them.

What are the "Corbetts" in your life? The things you're so afraid of that the only way to handle them is to fall deeper in the shadow of your Father?

In the book *The Highest Good,* Oswald Chambers said it this way: "The remarkable thing about fearing God is that when you fear God you fear nothing else, whereas if you do not fear God you fear everything else."

Additional scriptures for personal study:
    Exodus 20:6   Deuteronomy 2:25
    Romans 8:28   I John 4:16-21

How is God's glory revealed through not fearing?

 Are there any "Corbetts" in your life you haven't stood up to? If so, why haven't you let God back you up?

 We miss so much when we let fear consume us. What would your life look like without unhealthy fear?

USE THIS PAGE TO JOURNAL ABOUT WHAT GOD IS REVEALING TO YOU TODAY.

J O U R N A L

USE THIS PAGE TO JOURNAL ABOUT WHAT GOD IS REVEALING TO YOU TODAY.

Turn Your face away from my sins
and blot out all my guilt.
God, create a clean heart for me
and renew a steadfast spirit within me.
Do not banish me from Your presence
or take Your Holy Spirit from me.
Restore the joy of Your salvation to me,
and give me a willing spirit.
(Psalm 51:9-12)

Glory Revealed Through Sin

It's probably a safe bet that most people serving life sentences in prison have at least one thing in common: They didn't get there overnight. Little by little, smaller crimes led to bigger ones in a haze of circumstances that left the convict wondering, *How did I get here?*

Pick any prison cell, and the story of the person in it would sound strikingly similar. "It all started with a candy bar I took when I was seven. Some older kids dared me to do it. Then they dared me that I couldn't get a CD past the metal detectors. Then a leather jacket. Then a car. Finally one day, I broke into a house to score some real valuables. I didn't think the owner would come home. He did. I got spooked and shot the guy. Now I'm in prison for life."

Scandalous sin rarely starts as a premeditated choice to live blatantly against God's commands. More often than not, it's about a progression of small steps fueled by selfishness and pride—a lot of little sins that add up to a big downfall.

In the Bible, we see this no more clearly than in the life of David. David believed he had the skills and résumé to flirt inconsequently with disobedience. He thought he knew what he needed better than God did. What he really needed was to remain in a place of obedience regardless of his poster-child status.

King David was a bit of a roller coaster. One day he's one of the most heroic leaders of all time, the next he is committing a cowardly murder. One minute he's the greatest psalmist and songwriter who ever lived, the next minute he's a horrible father. David spent much of his life treading the line between obedience and disobedience. He was a man after God's own heart, yet a man after his own pleasure.

He's the Bible's original rock star—full of emotion, passion, and desire. But pair those qualities with a lack of discipline and you end up with a deadly cocktail. David was a great accident waiting to happen.

Ancient times demanded that kings be hands-on military leaders, personally waging war on the battlefield to lead their armies in victory and defeat. So when the time came for Israel to finish up a skirmish against the Ammonites, David did something uncharacteristic of a king—he sent his armies on while he stayed behind.

At first glance, this is so unlike the David we know. Isn't this the same little boy that single-handedly took on Goliath? How could it be that David the little shepherd boy was more of a man than the David we see here as a king?

Maybe the David who faced the giant was a little too celebrated—a spiritual prodigy who, over time, began to believe his own press. Could it be that he thought a little too highly of himself?

My theory is that David stayed behind in Jerusalem because he arrogantly thought a battle like this one was beneath him. It wasn't that he was afraid of the battle; he was simply bored with it. He probably thought, *Let my army fight. If they get into trouble, I'll ride in on my high horse and save the day!*

That attitude landed him in a very vulnerable place for failure. By deciding not to fight, David actually walked into the biggest war of his life—a war that his own unchecked pride and arrogance waged on himself.

One evening, miles away from his armies in battle, David is taking a kingly stroll on the palace balcony when the sight of a beautiful woman bathing on a rooftop arrests his attention. A more obedient David would have strolled right back into the palace, casting lust from his heart, but instead, we see him exercise a spectacular feat of disobedience. He summons his messengers to collect the woman, who, as it turns out, isn't just a stunning maiden. Her name is Bathsheba, and she's the wife of Uriah—one of the very soldiers out fighting David's battle.

When David commits adultery with Bathsheba, we witness what would seem to be the beginning of his great slippery slope. But the truth is, he was already on slippery ground without the right shoes! His attitude left him without the grip on reality he needed to return to a place of obedience, so naturally we see him start to fall. As a result of his flirtations with sin, David gets Bathsheba pregnant. And since her husband is away on the battlefield, someone's going to have a bit of explaining to do.

David is slipping faster with nothing to grab onto, so he starts taking out others on his way down. He decides to trick Uriah into believing he's the father of the baby. Under false pretenses, David calls him home from battle, giving him the opportunity to reunite with Bathsheba. It's a great plan... except that the loyal soldier doesn't bite. Uriah is such a patriot that he refuses the comforts of his own home—even at the urging of his king—when his fellow troops are suffering on the battlefield.

Now what? Apparently, Uriah is a noble man so firmly grounded that he won't easily fall into David's cowardly plan. So David, still slipping, tries desperately to grab Uriah from every angle, but nothing works. After a few more failed attempts, David decides the only solution left is to have Uriah killed in battle. In a move so heartless it could have only come from the very darkest of places, David asks Uriah to return to battle and dutifully deliver an envelope containing his own death decree.

Think back to that first evening on the roof. Was David already so far gone that he woke up thinking, *I wonder if I can find a woman whose husband I can have killed? To the rooftop!* Of course not. It almost never happens that way.

David's plan started out simple enough: Take a well-deserved break from battle. *Focus dims. Grip weakens.* Stop and stare at the woman, the naked married one. *Completely out of focus now, David's treads begin wearing out.* Have her over. *Slip.* She's pregnant. *Slipping faster. His shoes are ripping apart at the soles.* Then the cover-up. *Holding onto the side of the cliff, David grasping for anything, clawing to regain ground.* Then the murder. *Darkness.*

Somewhere along the line, David was so far into disobedience that he wasn't only giving into temptation, he was actively looking for more. Over time, he let his attitude get so out of check that the heroic shepherd-boy-turned-king found himself in a prime position for his lack of discipline and accountability to catch up to him.

In life we see the effects of disobedience creep up on us more often than not. It's the classic "frog in the kettle" story. Throw a frog in hot water, and you'll see just how high it can jump on it's way out of the pot. But place a frog in cool water, gradually turning up the heat, and it will stay put until its insides boil.

Why even flirt with sin in life? Just stay as far away as possible.

Sin works the same way. We wake one morning and decide to neglect God's principles, disobeying him in a "small" way. What's the big deal about a little lie? The next thing you know, you're telling a medium-sized lie to mask the little lie—something you'd have resisted the day before. In no time, you're creating scenes of deception so great you didn't even know you were capable of creating them. Even worse, your spiritual radar becomes so desensitized you may not even realize it.

I heard a story once about a wealthy man who'd just bought a pristine Bentley. He was elated about his new prize after being on the waiting list for a year. So he was extremely picky when it came to hiring his new chauffeur. He put three highly qualified applicants through a rigorous set of interviews and tests. Each candidate seemed equally capable, so the man came up with a tiebreaker.

He placed an orange safety cone in the middle of his helipad, instructing each driver to swerve as close as he could without hitting it. The first driver managed to get three inches from the cone without so much as tapping the breaks. Impressive! The second driver was even more masterful. He brought the car so close to the cone that the draft shook the cone from side to side—but he never actually hit the cone!

Everyone was a bit tentative as the third driver took the wheel. How could he possibly outdo the second driver without scratching the car? But the third driver didn't seem phased. Confidently, the chauffeur put the car in drive, stepped on the accelerator and drove clear across the helipad avoiding the cone by thirty yards!

Stifling chuckles, the owner of the Bentley asked the third candidate, "What in the world did you do that for? You didn't even come close to the cone!"

The chauffeur replied, "If the goal was not to hit the cone, I see no reason to flirt with it just to see how close I can get. If you hire me, I will stay far away from things that will harm your car so that I don't hit them."

He was hired on the spot. It's better to have the driver who's wise and guarded than the one who's flirtatious and arrogant.

Why even flirt with sin in life? Just stay as far away as possible. David's selfishness and pride had him fooled into thinking he was strong enough to come out clean on the other side of his hazardous encounters.

God said, "Go to battle."

David said, "No," due to selfishness and pride.

God said, "Don't covet another man's wife."

David said, "I can handle it," due to selfishness and pride.

God said, "Don't commit murder."

David said, "Sorry, I've got to take care of this," due to selfishness and pride.

David woke up with his heart in its own prison cell wondering, *How did I get here?*

The murder probably felt sudden and overwhelming, but the reality is that he'd been heading down a path of destruction for a long time.

God's glory is revealed by watching David submit to the consequences he knew he deserved. He had disobeyed the Lord, and caused himself and others harm. Throughout the painful time of discipline, David praised God and didn't struggle against his loving Father. David learned that he could either be a positive testimony by taking God's commands and consequences seriously, or he could be a negative one by resisting God's righteous discipline. Either way, God still would receive the glory.

It's a lot like a child who decides to disobey his parents because he thinks *I know better than you,* when he actually just can't see everything his parents see. That child will either pay the consequences by bringing harm to himself and others, or he'll pay the consequences of being intercepted by the loving wrath of his parents. From then on, that child will listen more closely to what they have to say.

When we find ourselves in situations brought on by our sin and disobedience, we need to listen more closely to what God has to say. We must put more weight on his commands—more stock behind his instruction. We learn to take his loving discipline soberly and submissively. And that's how he gets more glory.

There's one other way God's glory is revealed in this tragic situation. David, in his most unlovable hour, sees a God who still loves him. A God who will not leave his side. There were consequences to David's actions which are evident when we look at the tragic series of events following David's sin. However, it is also evident that God doesn't condemn David. David is eventually restored as a king who is scarred but smarter.

God's glory is revealed through the consequences of David's sin, and his glory is also revealed through his merciful love for a repentant king. A strong presence of God's discipline, mercy, and grace make David love God even more, want God even more.

Additional scriptures for personal study:

Micah 7:19-20	James 1:14-15
Hebrews 2:1-3	Romans 3:21-26

How is God's glory revealed through sin?

There are many moments we can point to when David went wrong, but when do you think he lost his sensitivity to obedience?

Where are the slippery slopes in your life—the times when you find yourself flirting with disobedience?

USE THIS PAGE TO JOURNAL ABOUT WHAT GOD IS REVEALING TO YOU TODAY.

USE THIS PAGE TO JOURNAL ABOUT WHAT GOD IS REVEALING TO YOU TODAY.

Turn Your face away from my sins
and blot out all my guilt.
God, create a clean heart for me
and renew a steadfast spirit within me.
Do not banish me from Your presence
or take Your Holy Spirit from me.
Restore the joy of Your salvation to me,
and give me a willing spirit.
(Psalm 51:9-12)

Glory Revealed Through Accountability

I'm a huge fan of horse racing. Horse racing is the epitome of beauty in motion—sheer power mixed with breathtaking excitement. If you visit my office, you'll see a good portion of wall space dedicated to vintage press clippings of a horse named Seabiscuit. It's a horse that, in the 1930s, took the world by storm and got more front-page headlines than World War II and Hitler combined. But that was a long time ago.

In 2006 the world of horse racing had a new headline story. A story, ironically, not about a horse and his victories but about a horse's downfall and the hero that saved his life. In the 2006 season, my hopes—along with the hopes of a nation—hung on a thoroughbred named Barbaro.

In horse racing, the equivalent of the Super Bowl is a series of three races known as the Triple Crown. It's a huge deal—to earn the crown one horse has to win all three races! The first race is the Kentucky Derby, followed by the Preakness, and finally, a race known as the Belmont Stakes. It's no small feat; there hasn't been a winner since 1978. So naturally, every year, there's great media speculation surrounding the winner at Churchill Downs, the home of the Kentucky Derby. Everyone brings up the billion-dollar question that haunts the victor—can he win the next two?

In 2006, Barbaro had us all abuzz. He didn't just win the Kentucky Derby, he took it by six-and-a-half lengths—the greatest margin of victory since 1946! When it came time for Barbaro's much-anticipated run for the second tier of the Triple Crown, the unthinkable happened.

Just strides into the race, Barbaro's right rear ankle snapped in a break so severe that Edgar Prado, Barbaro's jockey, heard an audible click and immediately pulled up on the reins.

They say that during a race, a horse is so full of adrenaline that he can't feel pain. He has only one thing on his mind—to run. In the moment of his injury, Barbaro, trained his whole life to think of nothing but surpassing the horses on either side, recoiled as Prado pulled on the reins. He protested, trying only to continue what was in his blood—keep going.

Can you imagine the intensity of the moment? Barbaro is confused. Not feeling any pain, he's probably thinking, I'm fine! Let me keep running! Can't you see we're in a race here? I thought we were both on the same team? Why are you pulling back the reins and sidelining me?

Prado, the jockey, stayed firm on the reins, desperate to keep the horse from further injury. He held on tightly until he was sure that Barbaro was reined into submission. He then let go, slid down off of the great racehorse's back, and using his full body weight, leaned in to support the broken Barbaro—all of this happening for the entire world to watch.

The hero of our story is God— he deserves all the glory.

On that day, the biggest story was not about who won the Preakness, but about tragedy and defeat. The focus of the world switched from whether or not we'd have a new champion to whether or not our fallen favorite would survive. Prado became the hero of the story, not by winning the race on a majestic horse, but by losing it on a broken one.

See, jockeys are animal lovers. Prado wanted to win, but not at the expense of allowing a horse he loved to run crippled. He knew that with every step, the horse was hurting himself even more. Prado knew that Barbaro might not understand why he pulled back so fiercely on the reins.

But it wasn't about keeping the horse happy; it was about keeping the horse alive.

As it turns out, Barbaro's injuries were life threatening. His leg was broken in three different places. Had Prado not acted so quickly, it's likely that Barbaro would have been euthanized on that very track. While it's almost certain that Barbaro will never run on a racetrack again, six months, twenty-seven screws, and a case of laminitis later, the one certain thing was that he was still alive.

Since that infamous afternoon at the race, there has been so much press about the horse, the owners, and the heroic and wise jockey. There is, however, one angle of Babaro's story that the press has neglected to cover: the leather reins.

It's interesting that no one's done a story about the leather reins that Prado used to stop Barbaro in his tracks. The reins could have snapped under the pressure. They could have unbuckled and failed the jockey. But they did exactly what they were created to do—obey the jockey's command. As much as adrenaline-filled Barbaro would have wanted them to let him continue to barrel down the track, the reins didn't give out. They probably even bloodied the horse's mouth when the force of Prado's command pulled Barbaro to a full stop.

Barbaro reminds me of what people must have thought of King David in the Bible: Gorgeous. Fast. Everyone's favorite for the crown. Yeah, maybe even a little cocky!

In Psalm 51, we see the aftermath of a celebrated king running on his own confidence, thinking he couldn't lose. He loved the thrill of the run, the thrill of the chase—he loved to win. Then came the break. One bad step lead to another, and the king found himself in a world of turmoil. While he should have stopped after the first sign of trouble, David kept running. Full of egotistical adrenaline, he stayed on his perilous track, compounding his injuries with each new sinful step. But God, in his great mercy, pulled the reins and stopped David from ultimate destruction.

The hero of our story is God—he deserves all the glory. But the prophet Nathan deserves a few minutes of reflection here as well. See, in parallel to the Barbaro story, God, much like Prado, used Nathan as the rein to pull David from further harm. The most loving thing God could have done was to get David off of that track, even if he had to bloody David's mouth. And Nathan was the harness that God used to help lead David to a position of brokenness and repentance.

When God called Nathan to confront David and hold him accountable,

Nathan could have snapped under the pressure. But instead he did what was hard—he obeyed. Knowing that David would not be happy once he felt the bit tighten, Nathan approached his friend gently and wisely. After all, he was just a prophet in David's kingdom and as king, David had the power to end Nathan's life. But what Nathan clearly understood was that God's priority wasn't keeping either of them happy; God wanted to use Nathan to rein David in.

Armed with wisdom from God, Nathan approached his king with a parable he knew would get his attention. He told the former shepherd a tale of a rich man who'd stolen a poor man's pet lamb so that he wouldn't have to slaughter his own. David became furious at the story and demanded Nathan see to it that the rich man be punished. When Nathan revealed that the rich man in the story was actually David, and his sins were the same, we finally see our king safely reined in from his own demise.

David's response was complete brokenness. He could have lashed out at Nathan, but instead, he held tightly to God. He understood that Nathan was just a brave messenger and that ultimately, God was the one confronting him with his sin. He cried out to God in repentance and in a place of undeniable brokenness, asking to be restored.

In the story of Barbaro, we see the stern love of a jockey revealed in the pull of a rein. In the story of David, we see the love of God revealed through the obedience of Nathan. Here, God reveals his glory through accountability. He uses Nathan to confront and expose David. And David, recognizing God's pull, doesn't switch blame or lash back at Nathan. How silly would it have been to destroy the rein that Prado used on Barbaro the day of the race? If anything, that rein should be a treasured possession.

Months later, I was watching the news and saw an update segment on Barbaro. There was the great runner, barely walking, but walking all the same. Fully restored? No. But restored? Yes.

There, walking beside him was Prado, holding a rein. I wondered if it was the same rein as the one used the day of the race.

The segment wasn't as much about the greatness of the horse as it was about the greatness of the restoration. From brokenness, there came an opportunity live another day. It would be an understatement to say that the story was very revealing and beautiful.

I thought of David in Psalm 51, when through accountability, brokenness, restoration and love... God's glory was revealed.

Sadly, Barbaro did not ultimately survive the incident. Months after his fall, he had to be euthanized. This might not be the Hollywood ending we were all hoping for, but the extra 254 days that Barbaro lived past the day of his fall were 254 revelations of grace. Undeserving days given to him thanks, in part, to Prado: The jockey that bloodied his mouth out of love.

Additional scriptures for personal study:
Romans 8:1 1 John 1:8-9
James 4:7 Proverbs 27:17

How is God's glory revealed through accountability?

What do you think loving accountability really looks like? If you knew you needed to be the reins for someone whom God was pulling back, what would you do?

Think back to a time when you were sidelined by God. Did you take the time to really heal? Did you do everything you needed to do to be restored? Search your heart—is there still room for restoration?

USE THIS PAGE TO JOURNAL ABOUT WHAT GOD IS REVEALING TO YOU TODAY.

For you will forget your suffering,
recalling [it only] as waters that have flowed by.
(Job 11:16)

Glory Revealed Through Suffering

Dear Friend,

I'm reaching out to you from eternity to let you know that you've been heavy on my heart lately. I've noticed a lot of suffering, despair and loneliness around you. It's obvious that you live in a world of hurt.

It's not that in my day there wasn't suffering—we had plagues, wars, and disasters then, too. It's just that you'd think with all the technology and medicine available to you now that things wouldn't be in such bad shape. And it seems it's just getting worse all the time.

- 820 million people on earth go to bed hungry every night. That number doesn't get smaller—it grows by four million every year.
- 200 million of your children are homeless.
- 143 million are orphans.
- Every six seconds, someone is infected with HIV. Every five more, someone will lose their battle with it.

- Every other second, an unborn baby is legally terminated. No one knows how many die illegally.
- 2 million children have been sold into sexual slavery, while 250,000 children are enslaved as child soldiers on real battlefields.
- And roughly once a decade, a race of people almost disappears because another race decides, for whatever reason, they don't deserve to live.

I know what you're thinking. *The third world is a scary place. A place filled with suffering.*

Yes, there are places in Africa, Central America, and Asia where poverty levels are high and the quality of life is dismally low. But consider what happens in the world's wealthiest nation. A country that prints "One Nation Under God" on its currency:

- 37 million live in poverty, choosing between turning on their heater or feeding their children.
- 7.5 percent of young girls starve themselves because they believe they're too ugly to eat.
- 17,000 people are killed in drunk driving accidents every year.
- 17,000 children are injured in school bus accidents every year.
- 1 in 4 women will be sexually assaulted in their lifetime. For men, it's 1 in 6.
- 43,000 of your mothers, sisters, and daughters will die from breast cancer.
- And one out of every two marriages will come to a bitter end.

The fact is, suffering will always be with us. It's an inescapable reality that comes with living on this planet. Bad things will happen, and we will do what we can to prevent them. But not all bad things come as a result of sin in our lives, and finding yourself in the middle of suffering without explanation is one of the loneliest places imaginable.

My name is Job, and for a couple of millennia now, I've been the go-to guy for unexplained suffering. There's an entire book in the Bible dedicated to my plight because it wasn't an easy one to understand. See, I wasn't your stereotypical victim. I wasn't poor, or leading a fringe life in a forsaken corner of the world. I was a wealthy, righteous man, secure in my faith and honorable to all who knew me.

In one fateful moment, I lost almost everything I had—my cattle, my servants, even my children. As if that wasn't enough, some sort of affliction began eating my flesh, and I was covered in boils from head to toe.

My initial reply was one of faith. I fell to my knees and uttered the infamous line, "The LORD gives, and the LORD takes away. Praise the name of the LORD" (Job 1:21 KJV). My wife began to curse God for allowing these things to happen to me, and still, I stood firm. I believed that God knew what he was doing. It wasn't until several well-meaning friends tried to triage any hidden sin in my life that my spirits began to unravel.

The thing is, God wasn't punishing or disciplining me for anything that I did wrong. Far from it. He was actually reshaping and molding me to become more reliant on him—to trust him more. God's hand was at work the whole time with plans and purposes far beyond my understanding; who was I to question him? Was I there when the foundations of the earth were laid? Had I ever given orders to the morning or shown dawn it's place? Did I set up the laws of the heavens? No!

How arrogant is it for us to presume that we understand all of God's plans? Or that he owes us some sort of report clearly stating his agenda? Isaiah 55:8 says: "For My thoughts are not your thoughts, and your ways are not My ways." At the same time, Romans 8:28 says: "We know that all things work together for the good of those who love God: Those who are called according to His purpose." That doesn't mean for the apparent good obvious to our feelings every moment of the day—but for our eternal good.

Suffering is a blessed fact of life!

I can personally testify that suffering is a gateway through which I learned to desperately long for God. To depend on him. To be reminded of how much I needed him. God needed me to need him more, and he had to strip everything that I called "mine" away to get me there.

James 1:2-4 says: "Consider it a sheer gift, friends, when tests and challenges come at you from all sides. You know that under pressure, your faith-life is forced into the open and shows its true colors. So don't try to get out of anything prematurely. Let it do its work so you become mature and well-developed, not deficient in any way" (MSG).

Suffering is a blessed fact of life! No one is immune. Just as sure as jumping in the middle of a river ensures you will get wet, living in this world ensures hardship and pain will come your way. If, by chance, you've gotten this letter and you haven't had any suffering yet—just wait. The question is not if, but when and how often! Recognizing this truth doesn't make you a pessimist, it makes you a realist!

Here's another reality: The questions won't go away once trials come.

WHY!? I thought God was a loving God. A good God. A just God. Why is life breaking down?

These are questions that are almost impossible to put to the side in the middle of our pain. But the simple answer is that we live in a broken world—the land of the dying. Suffering reminds us of just how fallen this world is. That this is not our home. It instills in us a longing for heaven. A longing for a place where there will be no tears, no hunger, no homeless children. It also draws us near to God. It begs for us to lean on him in times of instability.

I can promise more prayers are said from war bunkers than safe suburban homes. More commitments of faith are made in waiting rooms of hospitals than at award ceremonies. Don't believe me? Look at the times in your life when hardship came at you like a hurricane. Maybe you lost something great, but you gained a new reliance on God. And in that moment, his glory was revealed by being your anchor in that storm.

When the story of my life was said and done, it was hardly all sunsets and rainbows. Had it been, you probably would never have heard of me. Yes, God allowed me to have another family, and he restored my wealth to greater levels than I'd ever seen. But I never again got to hold in my arms the children I lost. I never got back the time that I spent in agony and despair. What I got instead was God and God alone. And I can tell you now, he is everything I need.

Should this letter find you in the middle of your darkest hour, I pray you remember that our God has you firmly in his hand. You are your strongest when you cling to him. Trust him, he has your ultimate good in mind. You can take my word for it—I've been there.

At home,
Job

Additional scriptures for personal study:

Isaiah 55:8-9	Romans 11:33-35
Romans 7:15-25	Psalm 135:6

How is God's glory revealed through suffering?

 Think of the times in your life when suffering hit you the hardest. What kind of work did God do in you during that time? What was he teaching you through it?

 Let's pretend you have a friend who is struggling to make sense of the tremendous suffering in the world. This struggle is hindering her from pursuing a relationship with God. How would you approach her? What would you say?

USE THIS PAGE TO JOURNAL ABOUT WHAT GOD IS REVEALING TO YOU TODAY.

USE THIS PAGE TO JOURNAL ABOUT WHAT GOD IS REVEALING TO YOU TODAY.

For you will forget your suffering,
recalling [it only] as waters that have flowed by.
(Job 11:16)

Glory Revealed Through Friendship

Not all Christmas mornings are filled with laughter and cheer. For me and my wife, one Christmas was especially hard.

Try staring at a stocking hanging from the chimney, full of toys and gifts for a little boy who wouldn't be home to open them. A little boy that Jennifer and I had worked tirelessly to adopt. A little boy stuck in another country by red tape that neither he nor we could understand. His name was Rudy.

When Jennifer and I started the process of adopting Rudy, a five-year-old boy orphaned in Guatemala, it was only supposed to take four to six months. Supposed to. Instead, we spent twenty-one months of sleepless nights and countless tears preparing for his arrival. The cost was much more than originally planned, both emotionally and financially. We had our faith and our hearts tested in ways we didn't think possible—all in a fight to bring our son to his new home. It was hard, but it was worth it.

We had lots of great friends surrounding us, praying for us and for Rudy. But nothing seemed to be going our way. Home studies expired while fingerprinting and background checks inexplicably had to be redone. For a time the Guatemalan government put an indefinite hold on all adoptions and, to top it all off, some of our paperwork got lost and we had to start much of the process all over again. Here we were trying to do something we knew was so right, but something was going wrong at every turn. Every day we would wake up and hit a new obstacle.

In the middle of that twenty-one month season, I had a conversation that I will never forget.

I had just finished speaking at a conference in Nashville, Tennessee. During the message, I shared with the group our uphill battle to bring our little boy home. I asked the crowd to pray for us as we stayed the course. Afterward a lady and her husband asked if they could speak to me privately. We went backstage, and that's when the couple began what felt more like an interrogation than a conversation.

"I think I know how to get your son home ASAP," the man told me.

That got my attention. I was all ears. Until they explained.

They asked if there were any unconfessed sins in my life. They went on, explaining that it was likely those unresolved sins that were keeping Rudy from coming home.

"God is punishing you, and only you know why. You just haven't confessed it, and your dishonesty is costing you," they continued.

I guess they thought that surely there was some big hidden sin in either my or Jennifer's life that would explain everything we were going through. As soon as we would repent, the floodgates would open and the hard days would be over.

What a hard thing to hear!

I assured them that yes, I am a sinner, and that Jennifer was no exception. I also thanked them for taking the time to come and talk and that I would look deeper within to see if there was any unresolved sin I needed to confess. We then prayed together—but here is the weirdest thing about it all: I had a hunch that the couple was disappointed in my prayer. I couldn't help but think they were hoping to hear some juicy confession.

I remember sitting there afterward thinking to myself, *They meant well, but they just don't understand.*

In one sense, they were right—God was using the situation to confront me about my pride. But in another sense, they were wrong to presume that it must have been my actions that kept a little boy fatherless. I realized that they were trying to help. As a matter of fact, the question was a valid one to ask. We all need to daily examine our lives and bring our failures to the foot of the cross, but in this case, they were missing the point.

At that moment in my life, God was not punishing me, He was enlarging my dependency upon him. He was stretching my faith so that he could strengthen it.

It's one of the hardest things in the world when we see someone we love suffering.

This is how Job must have felt throughout his struggle. Well-intended people gave him good advice that just missed the mark. Job's advisors assumed that there must have been sin to bring on well-deserved punishment. With the best of intentions, they started troubleshooting when, in all honesty, it was a classic case of the right advice at the wrong time.

Job's scenario wasn't one where he'd blatantly disobeyed God. This was not King David needing Nathan to come in and speak graceful rebuke. Job was a righteous man who had hard times come upon him in his most obedient days. Job wasn't perfect—he had issues with pride—but he wasn't living a prodigal life. He was simply a good man, doing good things, and then bad things started to happen.

What Job needed from his friends was support. More than an examination and prescription, Job just needed a hand to hold.

This was precisely what we needed, too—we needed support! We needed someone to hold our hands and cry with us. To pray with us. To share the load of our suffering. All we wanted to do was bring a little boy home who had no mommy and daddy, and here in the middle of our pain was a couple trying to triage us.

Sadly, this happens a lot in the church. I know—I've been guilty of doing it myself.

When life hits the fan, sometimes well-intentioned people feel like it's their obligation to give advice. They love us so much that they can't just leave us in our pain. But sometimes their advice, while sounding godly enough, entirely misses the mark. It's good advice but applied to the wrong situation at the wrong time. And in the process, they end up compounding our suffering with confusion.

It's one of the hardest things in the world when we see someone we love suffering. It's even harder to watch them and do nothing. Hugs don't feel substantial enough. Tears don't feel like they make a difference. We want to fix the problem, fix them—fix anything! We give a godly shoulder rub, start singing "Friends Are Friends Forever," and try to give them a spiritual tourniquet to stop the bleeding.

Remember Job's friends with their less-than-righteous advice? On the surface, it sounded good and logical. Job was suffering so terribly that he must have somehow earned his affliction, right? He *had* to be in the wrong. They were only trying to troubleshoot his situation, and they loved him enough to be persistent and tough about it. But they were so off-base that God rebuked them for menacing a suffering man.

Author and teacher John Piper has a great point about what was actually going on here. Elihu, the fourth friend, had great insight for Job's situation. God allowed Job to suffer not to punish him for any sin, but so that he could refine his righteousness. It brought out a hidden condition in his heart— pride. Because God had Job's complete attention, Job could rely on God as he never had before. And through the process God got the glory!

Never miss an opportunity to shut up.

When we pull out our spiritual calculators and try to figure the equations adding up to the suffering of those we love, we actually do them a great disservice. It's like trying to squeegee the floor of a house while the floodwaters are still rising! God is still working in their hearts, and all we can do is stand with them until he's done. But we want so badly to run in and troubleshoot, especially after time passes and nothing is improving. When our friends are going through an earthly hell brought on by God-ordained circumstances, we don't need to be so quick to rush in and try to fix things. Sometimes the last things they need are big spiritual answers or armchair quarterbacks telling them where they went wrong. They need our friendship, support, and comfort. They need us to righteously shut up.

This is hardest for people like me. I'm a planner—a fixer—and in many ways, I give advice for a living. Prophecy is my calling! So imagine how hard it is for me to just shut up and not have an answer. Thankfully, the suffering I experienced through our trials with Rudy taught me a new perspective.

How ridiculous are these thoughts?

Maybe if I plant a seed and sponsor more World Vision kids everything will work itself out.

If I sing louder in worship, praising God for his goodness, he will notice my attitude and reward me with Rudy's homecoming.

Maybe I missed God on the whole adoption thing. Maybe we should have never tried.

As ridiculous as they sound now, they are actual thoughts that went through my head in the midst of it all. I didn't need any church people confirming these thoughts—I needed friends to remind me that God is at work, and that I can trust him in this journey.

Overall, God softened our hearts and let us realize how we needed him more than we needed Rudy home. Jennifer and I had to be brought to the point that desiring God and his will took precedence over desiring a good outcome to our situation. We had to rely entirely on Christ.

Thanks to the long wait, we also saw our parents go from being entirely lukewarm to the idea of adoption to longing for Rudy's homecoming with us. Our daughter, Grace, got to spend a little bit more time getting our full attention so that she was ready to add an older sibling and not resent his arrival. We also elevated our friendship with several people as they quietly stayed by our side—not preaching, not fixing—just lending support and being a safe place to vent once in a while.

God got more glory out of that hard season than most of our easier days. He revealed himself through so many friends. Sometimes through their tears and sometimes through their silence. Often they would just sit and pray with us. Sometimes they would send a note of encouragement or flowers, just because. We saw the graciousness and love of God through our friends when they would stop by with a stack of pizzas and a case of Diet Coke, with no agenda other than to make sure we didn't have to cook dinner. They'd babysit our little girl so that Jennifer and I had time for a night out. Friends collected a love offering to help with the enormous circumstantial expense of this adoption.

God loves community. God himself is community—Father, Son, Spirit. He certainly didn't have to create us, but he did. And He is delighted when we take care of each other by wearing robes of his character. His glory is revealed when we loving come alongside others through the hard times.

If you really want to watch God refine the hearts of those who love him, stand beside them in their suffering and watch his glory revealed.

And never miss an opportunity to shut up.

Additional scriptures for personal study:

| Matthew 22:36-40 | 1 Corinthians 8:2-3 | Isaiah 45:7 |

How is God's glory revealed through this kind of friendship?

Think of all of the places you've walked with people through their suffering. Were there times when you were less than a good friend? If you could revisit the situation, would you do anything differently?

How can you tell the difference between suffering brought on by sin and suffering brought on by circumstance?

JOURNAL

USE THIS PAGE TO JOURNAL ABOUT WHAT GOD IS REVEALING TO YOU TODAY.

Why am I so depressed?
Why this turmoil within me?
Put your hope in God, for I will still praise Him,
my Savior and my God.
(Psalm 42:5)

Then I will come to the altar of God,
to God, my greatest joy.
I will praise You with the lyre,
God, my God.
(Psalm 43:4)

CHAPTER 9

Glory Revealed Through Declaration

I often love to start out a worship service by getting people on their feet and asking them to shout out specific attributes of God. I say, "What has God been to you? Who has he revealed himself to be?" But most importantly, I ask them, "Who do you need him to be?"

I do this because there is so much power in declaration. Power in rehearsing the things you may not *feel* at the moment but you know are true. It's because simply saying out loud the things you need to hear goes a long way in preparing the spirit for things to be that way. It's the power of the tongue.

Psalm 42 is most famous for, "As a deer longs for streams of water, so I long for You, God." But it goes on to say, "My tears have been my food day and night, while all day long people say to me, 'Where is your God?'" (v. 3). Not the content of your average worship song.

Most psalms are songs of lament and honesty, but we don't hear about those too often. The ones written from the mountaintops of life tend to win popularity contests. But some of the most useful truths are in the psalms written from the valleys.

Lament is a powerful tool that God uses to draw us nearer to him. A while back Michael Card gave an interview in *Christianity Today* that really struck me. The whole interview was about sorrow, lament, and suffering—not something we read about a whole lot. A series of events led Michael to a season in his life pondering the mystery of suffering and what God's role was in it. He came to the conclusion that we can't understand God's worth without experiencing woundedness. God's worth is found in the desert, not in the picnic grounds.

Michael tells a story of a pastor friend who was paralyzed in an auto accident while out on a pastoral call. There was no obvious rhyme or reason to the tragedy—it just happened. When his friend began to cry out to God and experience his presence, his cries changed. "You don't have to heal me. Just don't leave me!" His friend learned that the presence of God was much more vital than God's provision.

What would happen if, in the middle of our lament, we grasped that God was really what we needed? What if our sorrow turned to declaration about his goodness? What if we ignored our feelings and, with our lips, moved on to the part where we honor God for everything that he is?

Alone, discouraged, finding himself clearly at the bottom, King David was dangerously close to giving up. He could have stuck his head in the sand and prayed for the buzzards to come and deliver him from his misery. But instead, he gave himself a wake-up call. David picked himself up by the bootstraps and ordered himself to place his hope in God.

> *Why am I so depressed?*
> *Why this turmoil within me?*
> *Put your hope in God, for I will still praise Him,*
> *my Savior and my God. (Ps. 42:5)*

Here was David in the middle of depression and despair, and the psalmist is actually preaching to himself. He more or less says, "This is not how I feel right now, but this is how I am." Our feelings are fickle, but our God is constant. Sometimes you just have to rehearse the truth out loud.

It always comes as a shock to many newlyweds that wedded bliss can be short lived. The mystery and wonder of courting rolls silently into the excitement of an engagement. The wedding is the pinnacle of beauty, ideals, and expectations sealed with the honeymoon. As beautiful as the whole process is, it's also an emotional sugar-high of romance and affection that eventually levels off at the first real-life fight, leaving the new couple feeling a bit dazed and hung over by the whole ordeal.

Marriage isn't meant to make us happy; it's meant to make us holy.

Couples begin to learn the real meaning of love and commitment when we face the everyday reality of sharing our lives with another human being. It's saying "I love you" when really for a fleeting moment you're hoping that your spouse gets lost on the way back from the grocery store. It's stopping to pick up take-out sushi for your wife when all you care about is getting your order of hot wings before the kick-off. It's putting away your make-up bag so your husband can have a countertop to rest his razor on. It's holding your tongue when you have every right in the world to remind your spouse how much you've altered your life for his happiness.

Marriage isn't meant to make us happy, it's meant to make us holy. We learn so much about salvation and redemption as we work out our rough edges through our life's companion. If all of us married couples lived strictly by our emotions, the divorce rate would be 100 percent. That's because emotions are unreliable—they're fleeting. We can't base our relationship with our spouses on them, and we most certainly can't base our relationship with God on them.

Mature relationships aren't easily moved by emotions or circumstances. You trust and remember the ultimate good of the other person, and you choose to believe in those things over what's immediately apparent. In our relationship with God, it's just the same.

In a letter to a friend, Mercy Otis Warren, Martha Washington once wrote: "The greatest part of our happiness depends on our dispositions, not our circumstances."

How true is that statement! Life weaves and winds us through seasons of different circumstances and emotions. They are all very real, especially when we're in the middle of them. Keeping a positive declaration—one that acknowledges God's promises in spite of our current location—can be the difference between making it through the seasons armed with experience, or dying in the valleys.

Ecclesiastes 3:1-8 puts it this way:

> **There is an occasion for everything,**
> **and a time for every activity under heaven:**
> **a time to give birth and a time to die;**
> **a time to plant and a time to uproot;**
> **a time to kill and a time to heal;**
> **a time to tear down and a time to build;**
> **a time to weep and a time to laugh;**
> **a time to mourn and a time to dance;**
> **a time to throw stones and a time to gather stones;**
> **a time to embrace and a time to avoid embracing;**
> **a time to search and a time to count as lost;**
> **a time to keep and a time to throw away;**
> **a time to tear and a time to sew;**
> **a time to be silent and a time to speak;**
> **a time to love and a time to hate;**
> **a time for war and a time for peace.**

I find it interesting that right after weeping comes laughing. Right after the break down, there's a build up. Silence before speaking. Declaration can bring us from the very worst to the light at the end of the tunnel. Claiming his promises is like looking for daylight.

Eugene Peterson's *The Message* has a unique take on this passage in Psalms, "When my soul is in the dumps, I rehearse everything I know of you" (Ps. 42:6).

What is something you know to be true about God, but you need to say out loud because it's the last thing you feel he is? Do you need him to be your provider? Do you need him to be your comforter? Then from your lips thank him for all of the times that he's comforted you.

Say out loud the promises of who he is. It's one thing to yell out to the Giver when you've just been given to. But why not thank him when your needs haven't yet been met? Try praising him when it's the very last thing you feel like doing. Let his glory be revealed in you despite your circumstances.

Additional scriptures for personal study:

Psalm 55:16-23	Psalm 146:6
John 16:33	1 John 2:27

How is God's glory revealed through declaration?

What is something you know to be true about God, but need to say out loud because it's the last thing you feel that he's been?

David managed to find comfort in the Lord when he was alone and at the bottom. What do you turn to first in times of trouble? Do you find yourself turning to God? To other people? To distractions?

USE THIS PAGE TO JOURNAL ABOUT WHAT GOD IS REVEALING TO YOU TODAY.

J O U R N A L

USE THIS PAGE TO JOURNAL ABOUT WHAT GOD IS REVEALING TO YOU TODAY.

Why am I so depressed?
Why this turmoil within me?
Put your hope in God, for I will still praise Him,
my Savior and my God.
(Psslm 42:5)

Then I will come to the altar of God,
to God, my greatest joy.
I will praise You with the lyre,
God, my God.
(Psalm 43:4)

Glory Revealed Through Experience

I can always spot a local when I'm traveling. He's the guy sitting on the bench, hanging out at the convenience store. Maybe he's playing a game of cards or chatting up the cashier while holding a hot cup of coffee. There's an ease of familiarity about him in an outpost full of transient visitors. He's always good for a story or a friendly hello, but if you really want to see him come alive, just ask him for directions.

"Go up the highway until you see Wal-Mart (ever notice how all directions involve a Wal-Mart?). Turn left, and then just after the big green mailbox you'll see it. If you see the pumping station, the one that caught fire last year, you've gone too far..."

I'll take an experienced local over MapQuest any day.

Once you've been down a road and know its nuances, you're specially equipped to tell others how to navigate it. The things you have to say come alive over any roadmap—because you can speak with sensitivity to geography. You can look at a traveler pulling a trailer and tell them, "Wait, the grade on that road is too steep for towing that kind of equipment." Or, "You're going to need chains once you get up the mountain."

In life, God uses the sum of our experiences to minister to other people. If anybody can speak the truth, it's a guy who's been where the other person is going. Otherwise, it's just a guy giving advice. People who can draw from a well of experience tend to speak from a different place. In Psalm 42, King David was in the wilderness. He's speaking out of his own hurt and honesty, but he also knows that God can use this wilderness time to be glorified. He puts his soul on notice:

> *Why am I so depressed?*
> *Why this turmoil within me?*
> *Put your hope in God, for I will still praise Him,*
> *my Savior and my God. (Ps. 42:5)*

He knows that his situation is temporary, so it's time to move on and give the glory to God.

He knows that trials happen, but God is sovereign.

He knows that as soon as he gets to worshipping, his mind will be off of the temporary and on the eternal.

He knows this because he's been here before.

When you're in the middle of a wilderness, remember that God ordains us to go through certain trials so that the validity of our testimony can speak into the lives of others. He uses our scars as beauty marks—badges of honor that can be used as roadmaps for others to further his kingdom.

One of the greatest testimonies of the last century came from the late Corrie ten Boom. The ten Boom family was one of the outstanding Christian families during World War II who risked everything to help traffic exiled Jews to safety. They were one of the main hubs of the Dutch underground, so when they were caught, they were sent to death camps along with the Jews they were hiding.

Most people in the ten Booms' shoes would have considered their capture the end of their ministry. But despite the tearing apart of their family, Corrie and her sister Betsie continued to minister and pray for those imprisoned alongside them with only their good attitudes and a small Bible they smuggled in. They held secret worship services, prayed for the other women, and were able to give thanks to God in the most gruesome circumstances.

They even gave thanks for the fleas.

Yes, the two sisters, in their barracks, decided that they would methodically confess thanks for everything around them, including the fleas that infested the straw beds. Their circumstances were so dim that they could have chosen to give up, but they begged God to help them give thanks for even the horrendous things.

As it turned out, the fleas were the only thing between the sisters and further harm. The infestation of their barracks was so notorious that the camp guards refused to go in and inspect the bunks or the prisoners for contraband. They wouldn't even touch the women. Had their Bible been discovered, the sisters would have met immediate death.

Corrie emerged from the camp a lone survivor—Betsie passed away just one week before they were both to be released. Corrie was convinced that God allowed her to survive so that a message of hope could be spread throughout the world. She traveled to sixty-one countries to tell her tale of God's goodness against a backdrop of the fiercest circumstances. Her book *The Hiding Place* was a best seller and was turned into a movie of the same name. Corrie's experience earned people's attention because her testimony was a powerful one.

He uses our scars as beauty marks...

Most likely you're not reading this in a concentration camp, but maybe you're caught in the middle of a nasty divorce between two parents who haven't stopped loving you, but just don't love each other. It's doesn't make any sense now, but what if fifteen years from now you find yourself eye-to-eye with a teenage girl in the same situation? How much more capable will you be to help her and minister to her need than someone who's never experienced that particular struggle?

I never signed up to be "the guy" who gets the phone call any time someone comes close to leading a Muslim brother to Christ. But having been there, I know why I get the calls. I can speak with authority, conviction, and understanding that someone else may not be able to. Because of the road God led me down, I have a responsibility to share the insight I have with others who find themselves on that road.

Sometimes, God can use even our mistakes as a warning sign to others.

We can share our scars with them by saying, "Don't go down these roads—look what happened to me!"

My dad told me a fable when I was a kid about a village wise man. Everyone respected him near and far—everyone went to him for advice. One day a little boy asked him, "How did you become so wise."

The wise man responded, "Come with me, I'll show you."

They walked through the streets of the village, hand-in-hand, until they came upon the village drunk. The wise man stopped and pointed to the man, passed out in the street.

"This man and I grew up together on the same street with the same kind of family and the same opportunities. He happened to be a few years older than me, so I looked up to him at first—following his every move. As time went on, he started getting in trouble. I learned that all I had to do was watch him first, and then do the opposite. That's how I became a wise man."

People can learn valuable lessons from the mistakes you've made. Just as some scars can be used as roadmaps, other scars can be warning signs. They can be used as a cautionary tale of what not do.

Maybe you were the girl who tried to hide her abortion, only to have your parents rush to the hospital when it went badly. Were you the guy who's health was so damaged by drug-abuse that you'll have nervous twitches and heart problems for the rest of your life? Did you let an eating disorder get so out of control that your friends caught you hiding silverware up your sleeve in restaurants to gag yourself in the bathroom? You know the realities of these pitfalls better than any public service announcement. Put your testimony to use and watch how profoundly God is glorified!

Short of being a prophet, if anyone can speak truth, it's someone who's been there. You won't be preaching from an empty soapbox when you've overcome the obstacles in your life by hanging onto and declaring the promises of God. When you remind yourself to get through your circumstances by having faith in the goodness of God, he sets you up to reveal his glory.

Additional scriptures for personal study:

Psalm 42   Philippians 2:14-18

Philippians 3:8-10

How is God's glory revealed through your experiences?

What are the wildernesses you've walked through that uniquely equip you to speak into the lives of others?

Think of a testimony you've been impacted by. What was it about that person's story that revealed God's glory?

USE THIS PAGE TO JOURNAL ABOUT WHAT GOD IS REVEALING TO YOU TODAY.

J O U R N A L

USE THIS PAGE TO JOURNAL ABOUT WHAT GOD IS REVEALING TO YOU TODAY.

The LORD is my strength and my song;
he has become my salvation.
This is my God, and I will praise Him,
my father's God, and I will exalt Him.

LORD, who is like You among the gods?
Who is like You, glorious in holiness,
revered with praises, performing wonders?

You will lead the people
you have redeemed with Your faithful love;
you will guide [them] to Your holy dwelling
with your strength.
(Exodus 15:2, 11, 13)

Glory Revealed Through Deliverance

There are stories in the Bible that are so complex, yet they're so simple in message. Stories that from beginning to end reveal a certain truth over and over again. Nowhere is that more evident than in the story of Moses as found in the book of Exodus.

In Moses's life, we see the fingerprints of God on every page. We see God delivering Moses as an infant, as a boy, as a teen, as a man, and even on his deathbed. His story is more about a faithful God than about a favored servant. As we look at this familiar text, let's read it with a magnifying glass, looking for the fingerprints of God. They will be hard to miss.

The second book of the Bible, the book of Exodus, is really the coming-of-age story of both the nation of Israel and also God's relationship with his people. It sets the background for how he relates to his own as we watch the relationship develop between the Creator and the formal organization of his people, the Israelites. It's a backdrop for the story of God's deliverance of those he loves and how he continues to take care of them even as they doubt him continually.

The Israelites were made up of twelve tribes. If you remember your Bible stories, Jacob—son of Isaac, grandson of Abraham—received the name "Israel" from an angel after an all-night wrestling match. Hence, Jacob's offspring became the twelve tribes of Israel.

But nations aren't formed overnight. It took time for the descendents of Jacob to multiply enough to become a people large enough to be reckoned with. It wasn't until a couple of generations multiplied that the children of Israel living in Egypt were of a large enough number to gain the attention of Pharaoh.

Concerned that this race of people would overpopulate and become stronger than his own, Pharaoh sought to oppress the growing Israelites, forcing them to become the laboring class of Egypt. This did nothing to control their growth—the more he afflicted them, the more they multiplied. Frustrated, annoyed, and intimidated by the thriving race, Pharaoh decreed that all male children of the Hebrews should be killed.

But God needed a leader for the forming nation of Israel. He needed a man who would unite the tribes and deliver them out of the hand of the Egyptians. To mold such a man, the Lord would have to deliver him over and over, revealing God's glory and faithfulness—leaving fingerprints of his intervention so unmistakable, that the man could lead his entire people to deliverance.

That man's name was Moses.

Moses was born to the tribe of Levi, which was the tribe of priests. At birth, his mother recognized him as a favored child and hid him away from Pharaoh's death decree. But she knew that she would have to give him up or he would be killed. She swaddled her baby in a woven basket, and in faith, let him drift away. The baby was eventually rescued from certain death by the daughter of Pharaoh, and God honored the faith of Moses's mother by impressing his mark on Moses's life from the very beginning.

Pharaoh's daughter fell in love with the child she found floating in a basket on the Nile and had mercy on him, knowing that he must have been a Hebrew. Ironically, the young child was raised in the palace of the very king who had decreed his death. But simply saving him wasn't a deep enough imprint for the man God had chosen to deliver his people—the princess hired the baby's very own mother to be his nurse, allowing young Moses to stay connected to his true identity and develop a love for his own people. God was putting his fingerprints all over the situation.

Years passed and, now a young man, Moses was walking about his adopted grandfather's kingdom when he saw an Egyptian beating a Hebrew. The plight of his own people came alive right in front of him as an enraged Moses lashed out at the Egyptian, killing him. Moses couldn't contain his anger—he had a passion for the Hebrews that God had put inside of him. When he killed the Egyptian, he knew that he would be leaving his place in the kingdom. Adopted into the royal family or not, the Pharaoh would certainly have him killed. So Moses went into hiding, fleeing to the land of Midian.

This time of being a stranger in a strange land could have been one of deep depression for Moses. Instead, God was busy continuing his work in Moses, ordaining a time of preparation for his great leadership. He gave Moses favor with the people. Moses married, fathered a child, and learned to become a shepherd while living removed from his people and his homeland. But it wasn't until God appeared to him in the form of a burning bush that Moses realized his true calling.

"Moses, Moses—remove the sandals from your feet. This is holy ground."

Moses hid his face from the bush, afraid.

"I am the God of thy father, the God of Abraham, the God of Isaac, the God of Jacob. I have seen the affliction of my people. I have heard their cry. I know their sorrow. And I have come down to deliver them."

A great leader can't lead where he hasn't been led before.

God reached out to Moses, the one he had already delivered, to deliver his people from Egypt. A great leader can't lead where he hasn't been led before. So Moses, marked from the very beginning by God's delivering hand, was well equipped to lead what would become the nation of Israel. He wasn't a skilled orator. He wasn't a great diplomat. He was simply a man who was a walking example of the value of redemption.

That's the kind of leader you want. A leader who can deliver, because he has been delivered himself. Moses was able to return to Egypt to deliver the Hebrews with power and authority given to him by God. Can you imagine what it must have been like to be Moses, after all of those years in exile, to not only set foot back into the kingdom but also immediately demand the release of an entire race? The very people who made up Egypt's entire workforce.

Moses had the confidence of the "I Am." The promise of a God who would allow him to perform miracle after miracle in the audience of a Pharaoh who wasn't willing to release the Hebrew people. In fact, Pharaoh just made their workloads harder, their lives even more tumultuous. But Moses persisted—he knew what it meant to be delivered and he was to soon see how God would deliver miracles through him.

Moses turned his rod into a serpent.

Pharaoh said no.

Moses turned the river into blood.

Pharaoh said no.

Moses released a plague of frogs.

Pharaoh said no.

Moses released a plague of lice and flies.

Pharaoh said no.

Moses released a plague killing all of the livestock of Egypt.

Pharaoh said no.

Moses afflicted the Egyptians with boils.

Pharaoh said no.

Moses called down hail upon the land.

Pharaoh said no.

Moses called a plague of locusts.

Pharaoh said no.

Moses allowed darkness to cover the land.

Pharaoh said no.

Finally came the plague we know as Passover, where the firstborn of every Egyptian family died. A plague so horrible that Pharaoh commanded Moses and his people to flee at once. He'd finally let God's people go... but only for a moment. As soon as Pharaoh realized that Egypt, already decimated by plagues, famine, and death, had just let their entire workforce escape, he had a change of heart.

Pharaoh immediately sent his armies after the fugitives to have them arrested and brought back into slavery. With the mountains to their right and a great body of water to their left, it looked as though the Israelites would be back working on the pyramids in no time.

But God had a different plan. A plan so dramatic that he turned to the one he knew he could trust. The one who already knew a thing or two about being delivered. He commanded Moses to lift his rod and part the Red Sea.

You know what happens next. It's one of the most epic scenes in all of the Bible—the stuff Hollywood movies are made of. Moses leads the Israelites safely to the other side of the Red Sea just in time to watch the Egyptian armies drown—horses, chariots, and all.

How could anyone, Israelite or Egyptian, deny the delivering power of God on that day? Was there any way to hide the glory of God through deliverance?

I like to think that was the moment that bonded the children of Israel. That they looked at each other and gave praise and thanks to God, and they realized just how special it was to be the children of "I Am." He brought to them a man named Moses, a baby with a death sentence, who was rescued from a river so he could deliver God's chosen ones from the hands of their oppressors and into the birth of their nation.

Now imagine you're Moses, on the far bank of the Red Sea. You've already seen the plagues. You've seen exile. You've seen the very hand of God spare your life over and over again. You're now witnessing first-hand the power of God to deliver an entire nation. You see that your life has been continually crafted by a God who's delivered you time and time again. Yet somehow you're still amazed at just how glorious he can be.

Along with the new nation of Israel, you sing:

LORD, who is like you among the gods?
Who is like you, glorious in holiness,
revered with praises, performing wonders?

Additional scriptures for personal study:
    Romans 8:15-17   Revelation 15:3
    Joshua 2:9-11

How is God's glory revealed through deliverance?

What are the things that you've been delivered from?

Through the life of Moses, we see God organizing a great setup. What do you think he's setting you up for?

J O U R N A L

USE THIS PAGE TO JOURNAL ABOUT WHAT GOD IS REVEALING TO YOU TODAY.

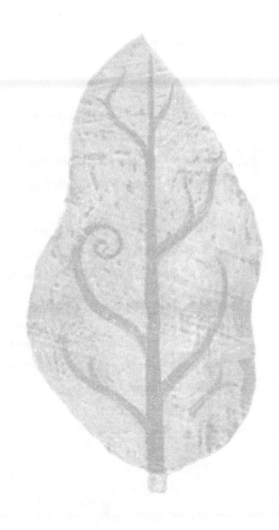

The LORD is my strength and my song;
he has become my salvation.
This is my God, and I will praise Him,
my father's God, and I will exalt Him.

LORD, who is like You among the gods?
Who is like You, glorious in holiness,
revered with praises, performing wonders?

You will lead the people
you have redeemed with Your faithful love;
you will guide [them] to Your holy dwelling
with Your strength.
(Exodus 15:2, 11, 13)

Glory Revealed Through Victory

They've just crossed the Red Sea. On foot. Pharaoh's armies, in hot pursuit just minutes ago, are no longer. They've drowned. The Israelites are officially free.

Having just witnessed the pinnacle of miraculous glory worked on their behalf, Moses and the Israelites stopped, celebrated, and gave thanks to the God who redeemed them. I can just see Moses beginning the chant, calling everyone to give God appropriate praise.

On the far side of the Red Sea, Moses was essentially saying, "God didn't bring us to this point so we can brag on ourselves and do whatever we want. No. He brought us to this point to make much of him. In this moment there is great responsibility—not to revel in our own glory, but to reveal his."

Everything in that statement sounds appropriate, right? The Israelites had clearly been delivered by the hand of God, and now they were giving him adoration. They gave glory where glory was due.

I wish it always worked that way.

How many times in life, at the end of Red Sea victories, do we remember to stop and give thanks?

How many times in the midst of great victory do we understand that there is a great responsibility to not get an enlarged head, but an enlarged heart for worship?

Have we celebrated the moment rather than the giver of the moment?

Do we get tangled up in looking at all the hard work that we've put in and give a little too much glory to ourselves?

Do our best intentions get run over by the sheer adrenaline of victory?

It's so easy to do. In our hearts, we try to be grateful for everything that God has done for us, but we get so overwhelmed by the emotions of our human nature that we forget to recognize that he's the one who delivers to us our victories—great and small.

Fame and power can serve as a sort of spiritual amnesia.

I love watching how different people handle Red Sea moments in their lives. My heart leaps at the end of an amazing college football game when, in the heat of the post game celebration, the star player attributes all of his team's triumph to the grace and glory of God. I'm always thrilled when someone at an awards ceremony makes honoring God the central focus of his acceptance speech or when a class valedictorian uses the moment, in front of all of her peers, to reveal the source of her strength and her success. It's always encouraging when a husband, fresh off of the news of a giant raise, calls his wife, not to beat on his chest, but to let her know that God's been faithful.

In all of these scenarios, it's people, in the middle of heady moments, getting it right. Giving glory where glory is really due. Taking whatever spotlight is shining on them and humbly turning it toward the God who gave them the light to begin with.

There is great spiritual maturity shown when someone praises God not only in the midst of their storms, but also at the end of great victory. Clinging to God in the difficult moments of life is hard, but celebrating him in moments of prosperity can be hard as well. When everything is going wrong, there is instant need for a God who is bigger than whatever we're facing. We tend to look for a God whom we can cling to in the hard moments of life. When we win, though, it's often very difficult to remember why we won in the first place. We lose sight of the fact that we won due to God's provision, that we are blessed because of his doing, not because of our own.

We see this time after time in the public arena. Fame and power can serve as a sort of spiritual amnesia. Someone becomes famous due to the gifts God has given them, but the more famous they become, the more self-oriented they become.

I know people firsthand that this has happened to. The good news is that I also know people who have not lost sight of the one who paved their road to success. One great example of this is a couple of guys known by their fans as "the two sexiest fat men alive."

The Rick and Bubba Show is a syndicated weekday morning talk radio show that originates from my hometown of Birmingham, Alabama. These two good ole' boys have grown their show from a local broadcast to a syndicated program being heard by tens of millions of people in nine states. This wouldn't be all that remarkable, except that these two guys dedicate a significant amount of time to talk about their faith. Not just faith-based issues or political hot-button topics, but actually talking about Jesus.

They feature ministers alongside Hollywood celebrities, Christian artists as well as rock stars, family and faith-themed discussions right next to jokes about the intern's dating life—all the while maintaining their hilarity and relevance to a secular audience. These guys are constantly making appearances on national television, interviewing luminaries, and continually growing their audience.

When you tune in, you realize that this might not be a Christian show on a Christian station, but it's definitely two Christian guys talking about everyday issues from a Christian perspective. Many of their listeners are not professing Christians, but that has not silenced these men about their love for Jesus. They never condemn a caller for having a different belief about God, and I have never heard them disrespectfully shove their views on anyone of any faith. They have, however, stood their ground. I have non-Christian friends who tell me they never miss the show. The humor and cultural relevance is why they tune in, but while listening, I know that ministry is happening. I call it ambiguously aggressive ministry! Occasionally, I have friends who listen and disagree with something that's said, and on occasion, I disagree with Rick and Bubba as well. But that has yet to result in my turning the knob.

Long before I knew these guys personally, I was a big fan. Through the years, I listened to them live their faith out loud on the airwaves. When the show started to grow in popularity, I have to admit, I began to worry. I remember thinking that if the audience gets too big, the spiritual content will probably get left behind. After all, the more broad the audience, the less particular the message, right? Wrong. These guys have done the exact opposite. Not only has the biblical content not been watered down, it's been turned up notch after notch, show after show.

Maybe you're reading this and thinking to yourself, *They are pandering to a particular audience. They're working the right-wing evangelicals all the way to the bank.* If that's the case, how do you explain the "Thirteen Working Days of Horror?"

Every October, in the days leading up to Halloween, the Rick and Bubba Show would feature a bit called "The Thirteen Working Days of Horror." The guys, alongside the show's producers (whom we all know as Speedy and Don Juan) and a few other personalities would visit haunted houses, chase goblins, and tell ghost stories. The listeners would tune in to laugh one second and be terrified the next. As far as radio goes, it was pure genius. It was also a huge hit!

As the ratings spiked, the advertising revenues around this bit grew as well. But the growth was bittersweet. The annual bit was a no-brainer in the avenues of ratings and advertising, but as Rick and Bubba were growing in their faith, conviction was beginning to set in. What was once not a big deal began to become one.

All of us who know them knew that the bit was only intended to be innocent fun. But at times it dabbled into spiritual warfare and accidentally made light of demonic forces. The majority of their audience loved Rick and Bubba's "Thirteen Working Days of Horror," but the guys only had God's opinion in mind.

Don't take my word for it; look at what they had to say themselves about the matter. They issued this statement on RickandBubba.com:

> Rick & Bubba's "13 Working Days of Horror" was simply a throw back to our days as kids, gathered around a campfire telling ghost stories trying to scare each other. It was for entertainment and humor purposes only, and was not meant as an endorsement of the occult, or to contradict our beliefs as Christians in any way. But as the stories went on, we felt it was drifting into an area we were not happy with. We began getting a lot of people almost obsessed with going out on hunts, and becoming more interested in the "spirit world."

Foremost, as Christians being very aware of spiritual warfare and as we have hopefully grown as believers, we found this segment hard to justify. We know it was very popular. We hope you understand our feelings to make this decision [to cancel this segment].

Generally, the more general-market you become, the bigger your audience gets and the more you're asked to dilute your faith. These two men choose the opposite of traditional thinking. They feel an even bigger responsibility to make sure that they tighten up their jokes and keep the content family-oriented. The bigger their audience becomes, the more dedicated they are to making sure God is honored, and that in honoring him, God's glory is revealed.

With great success comes great responsibility.

I appeared on their show one morning, and afterward they shared with me what was going on behind the scenes with "The Thirteen Working Days of Horror." They asked me and other ministers whom they knew personally to pray for them. Bubba called me two days later, after asking his pastor to speak into the situation. I'll never forget what he said: "God's already parted the sea for us. He's delivered this audience in front of us, and we want to be good stewards of it."

Rick and Bubba weren't standing on the far side of the Red Sea going, "Thanks, God, for getting us across the sea, we'll take it from here!" They were seeking his input. They were also not saying, "We'll praise you so that our audience will get bigger." They were simply saying, "God, we want to be obedient to you because who among the gods is like you, O Lord? You're majestic in holiness, working wonders on our behalf, and we want you to keep getting the glory."

With great success comes great responsibility. Rick and Bubba understand this. They're going against the grain of what's typical by making their show more and more God-centered. And they're not looking back. I could list for you pop singers who auditioned with their faith on their sleeves for Christian record labels, only to go mainstream and never mention Christ in their public lives. I've also watched celebrities begin to share their faith as part of their retirement plans. They live out successful careers in the mainstream without any public indication or fruit of their faith, but the moment the limelight starts to fade, they begin releasing Christian albums or working the Christian talk show circuits. It's almost as if God is an afterthought.

Now hear me carefully. I'm not passing judgment on the lives of others, and I praise God that some celebrities genuinely come to faith in Christ toward the end of their careers. I'm simply saying that we need to be careful not to ever put ourselves in a position to strip God of the glory he deserves—especially at the height of victory. Nor do I want us to forget the testimony of his great deliverance when things get tough.

We can also look to the Israelites for cautionary tales of what not to do. They got this victory right, but they had their share of glory hogging from there to the Promised Land. There was that episode where they complained about the manna—God's divine provision from heaven. Then there was that time when they built a golden calf, and Moses got so upset he broke the Ten Commandments in half. When things got tough, instead of remembering whose hand they were in, they lived on the Moses welfare plan, constantly whining and complaining for forty years!

We can learn from the Israelites and others by adopting a simple perspective shift. We need to naturally recognize God's goodness, no matter the context. In the great and the small, we need to remember that it's only because of his hand that we are where we are—and we need to give him the glory for it! If we constantly live with an attitude of thankfulness, no matter the situation, we'll be already trained to give him glory in the really big things. And after we remember him in the big things, the stain of his glory in our hearts will trickle back down into our lives the next time we're in front of a Red Sea that hasn't yet parted.

Additional scriptures for personal study:

Isaiah 12:2	Exodus 15:17
Psalm 55:18	1 Corinthians 1:26-29

How is God's glory revealed through victory?

Knowingly or unknowingly, in times of victory, have you ever stolen the glory from God? Why do you think you let that happen? Where was your heart? Where was your head?

Practice giving God the glory for the victories in your life big and small. Don't skimp. Take this time to give thanks for all of the struggles he allows you to win—even the ones you haven't won yet!

USE THIS PAGE TO JOURNAL ABOUT WHAT GOD IS REVEALING TO YOU TODAY.

USE THIS PAGE TO JOURNAL ABOUT WHAT GOD IS REVEALING TO YOU TODAY.

But He was pierced because of our transgressions,
crushed because of our iniquities;
punishment for our peace was on Him,
and we are healed by His wounds.
(Isaiah 53:5)

Glory Revealed Through The Cross

If I were to tell you right now that a blog had just been posted about you, I'm confident that you would immediately put this book down, log on, and do whatever you had to do to find it. You'd Google every relevant search tag to see what exactly had been written about you. When you found it, you'd read through slowly, taking in every word—savoring whatever it was about you that someone thought important enough to write about.

We all love it when nice things are said about us. I'm no exception. That's why I've got to admit that of all of the Scriptures in the Bible, Isaiah 53:5 is one of my favorites: "But He was pierced because of *our* transgressions, crushed because of *our* iniquities; punishment for *our* peace was on Him, and *we* are healed by His wounds." (emphasis mine). There are so many reasons I love this passage. Obviously it's a powerful, dramatic, and reflective verse dealing with the crucifixion of Christ. But what I love most is that it involves me.

When I study stories in the Bible—say, David and Goliath—sure, it relates to my life, but it doesn't address me directly. That's the beauty of this passage—it's so blatantly about me. It's about *my* sins. I deserve the wounds, the whip, the wrath. But somehow, by his wounds, I get *my* healing.

I love that. It brings the entirety of Christ's sacrifice into clear focus for me. It makes my salvation real. I deserve death, but somehow God saw fit to substitute his Son, living as real flesh and blood, to pay the price for me.

The reality of Jesus's crucifixion isn't something we should pull out of the closet once a year, dusting off for Easter ceremonies. It's much more personal than that. It's a truth we should live with daily—remembering Christ's sacrifice so that we take full advantage of our status as the redeemed.

So what I want to do is take the story of the cross and break it down detail by detail. Let's slow down, talk about the piercing, the crushing, the agony. But instead of looking at Christ going through the punishment, I want you to try putting yourself in his shoes. In the story below, you'll see places where I've left a blank. Insert your name in that blank. Pause, step by step, and try to grasp just exactly what Christ did in your place.

As you insert your name and begin to read, notice how everything in you tries to insulate yourself from engaging fully in the sacrifice. It's a normal disconnect. The truth is that we naturally don't want to participate in Christ's sufferings. Even if we did, we as sinful people could never understand the scope of what it means to fully embrace it.

As I went through this exercise, the most sobering aspect to me was not so much the reality that I was joining in the sufferings of Christ, but that I did not have the ability to fully engage. If all of this happened to me instead of Jesus, it would be a deserving punishment for a sinful man. We are told in 2 Corinthians 5:21 that, "He made the One who did not know sin to be sin for us, so that we might become the righteousness of God in Him." The power of the Gospel; the death, burial, and resurrection of Jesus Christ, is that he took the punishment that we deserved. He, the sinless one, took the punishment for our sin so that by trusting in him, we can escape eternal punishment and embrace eternal life. We can enter a relationship with the living God through the gate of Christ's sacrifice.

This is why I want us to start in the Garden—to remind us that the cross is so much more than just Christ taking our place for physical pain, but that he endured sin and betrayal with complete innocence in order to pay our penalty.

Ask yourself at each step: What is that like? How does it feel to be betrayed? If I had the power to stop it, would I? What does it mean to love and forgive the man who is beating me with a whip? Turn your wrist over—look at it. How would it feel to have a rusted nine-inch spike driven between your bones?

Isn't it ironic that we struggle with life being about our glory, right up until it comes to this moment? We want to play God and rule our own lives... until we're faced with being in Christ's shoes on that gruesome Friday. We live our lives struggling to let Christ be the Lord of our lives. We ignore him and try to save ourselves until we reflect upon the cross. All of a sudden, our perspective changes.

Sure the cross is all about me. It's about how I don't want it. It's about how even if I were willing to endure it all, it would be *me*, a sinful failure, paying the penalty for a judgment I deserve. It's about me only in realizing that he took my place, because I can't do it on my own.

Take the next few moments to read and reflect. The goal is not to replace ourselves with Christ, but to recognize that we couldn't if we tried.

I, _____, took the disciples to pray in the Garden of Gethsemane. I knew what they didn't—that even as I prayed, the chief priests and the elders were plotting my demise. I knew exactly what was ahead, and it was terrifying. I pleaded with God to take this cup from me. But I knew he wouldn't. It was his will.

I got up from prayer to find my disciples had left me entirely alone while they slept. Entirely alone on the eve of my darkest hour—but how could they know? I prayed even harder. With blood falling like sweat from my brow, I pleaded, "Father, if this can't pass away unless I drink it, Thy will be done."

Once more I found my disciples sleeping; once more I returned alone to pray. This is how I spent my last hours as a free man.

Suddenly, there was a commotion. Judas Iscariot entered the garden and greeted me with—a kiss? But behind him, soldiers were there for me. They arrested me, but not before Peter, waking from his slumber, jumped up and struck one with his sword, cutting off his ear. "Peter," I said, "He who lives by the sword dies by the sword." Such an irony—I, a non-violent man, would soon face the most violent death yet invented. The very soldier whose ear I healed led me off in chains.

Though it was my Father's will, I _____, was caught in the ultimate political crossfire. The counsel of Jewish leaders who had me arrested weren't actually in charge of Jerusalem. They were merely tolerated by the Roman government. But they were so afraid of me, afraid of how the people responded to me, that they had to find a reason to get rid of me before they lost spiritual control of the people.

The reasons behind my arrest were for "blasphemy," but the Jewish leaders knew that the Romans didn't care about such religious issues enough to sentence me to death. The priests had to up their charges against me, claiming that I had declared myself king—threatening the Roman throne—to even merit an audience with the Roman governor, Pilate.

Pilate knew I was an innocent man, but he had to keep his people happy. He balked at the charges and tried to release me. To him, I was just an unfortunate pawn in the power struggle between the priests and the government in a far-flung region of the Roman Empire.

He asked me, "Are you the King of the Jews?"

I had to be careful in my answer. I didn't care a thing in the world about an earthly throne, but I couldn't deny my spiritual one. Even though I was standing here in human flesh, I was the Son of God.

"You have said that I am," I replied.

Pilate was stunned that I wouldn't respond to any of the false accusations of the priests. Aside from treason, they accused me of endorsing tax evasion and inciting riots. None of these were true, but I wouldn't defend myself. At the very least, Pilate was expecting a religious lunatic—a crazy zealot—but instead, my words were few and non-confrontational. This was my burden to bear. But even as Pilate was amazed by how I handled myself, the crowds grew restless, and my fate as a traitor to the Roman Empire was all but sealed.

Pilate tried once more, at his wife's urging, to have me released. It was a custom to release a prisoner on this day—the day of a feast. Another political ploy to appease the Jews in the occupied land. Pilate brought out a notorious prisoner, Barabbas, hoping that the crowd would release me. Instead, their hatred for me grew louder. Hundreds of people yelled, "Give us Barabbas." They chose a horrible criminal to go free over me.

Out of the corner of my eye, as the soldiers led me away, I saw Pilate washing his hands. The last thing I heard as I was taken off to be beaten was, "Crucify _____."

The cries of the crowd were charged, but the Roman soldiers were just cold, calculated, and cruel. These were hardened professional killers. They led me to a whipping post where I was stripped naked. Over and over they pounded instruments of torture against my flesh—cutting, tearing, and ripping literal stripes of skin off my back. Veins were laid bare. Inner muscles and sinews were torn. That's what happened when they scourged me, _____, by whips embedded with glass, nails, and bone.

Careful not to kill me, for I still had a cross to bear, they put aside their whips—but only to make an absolute mockery of me. The soldiers, out of sport and boredom, covered my raw, burning flesh with a scarlet robe and placed a crown made of prickly thorns into my scalp. I was in physical agony, but they had the time to kneel before my shaking body and spit upon me like I was some village idiot. "Hail, King of the Jews," they sneered as my insides bled to the ground around me. If only they knew.

The physical break was short-lived. It was time for me to carry my cross. They might as well have asked me to carry my own coffin to the place of my burial. Still, I knew the burden was mine. I struggled with the weight of it for some time, but ultimately I fell to my knees. Another man had to help me finish the journey up to Golgotha.

When we got to the top of the hill, they offered me wine mixed with myrrh to dull my pain and my senses. There was still so much suffering ahead; they needed to make sure I was able to tolerate all of it. I refused. I needed to be sober. I needed to bear this pain. The sins of the world were to be atoned by my suffering. I, _____, needed to feel every excruciating moment.

What they did next was the most horrible torture mankind had yet devised. Crucifixion was designed to kill by way of slow suffocation. As the arms and legs of most victims were bound, the upper body would lose it's strength, eventually collapsing the weight of the body onto the lungs. But instead of letting my body collapse onto itself, they drove spikes through the bones of my wrists—adding extra support and extra time to my suffering. They nailed my feet into the cross so that I could stand longer.

As I hung there from my own limbs, I _____, suffered the effects of any human body exposed to such trauma. The arteries in my head and stomach were pounding. The insufferable thirst of being hung in the sun fueled the fever brought on by the swelling of my wounds. Tetanus began to set in from the rusty nails, and the wounds from which I was hanging tore further as my body shook harder and harder.

Yet, I never lost sight of my purpose on that cross. Even as the soldiers gambled my garments away while I hung there convulsing, even as they hung a mocking sign above me reading, "This is _____, the King of the Jews," I still kept my character. On either side of me were true criminals—thieves being crucified for their crimes. One of them was defiant, mocking me, daring me to come down off of my cross. How much I wanted to.

The other criminal understood who I was. He asked if I would remember him when I came into my kingdom. Of course I would. I wonder if he knew how he reminded me, in my weakest hour, what I was there for.

Then more hours passed as I, _____, hung in agony, the sins of the world gnawing on every nerve in my flesh. It was now that I realized that even God the Father couldn't look upon me. I cried, "My God, My God, why hast thou forsaken me?" The people still there thought I was confused and filled a sponge with sour wine, pushing it up to my lips.

As soon as the wine touched my lips, I knew the cup had passed. "It is finished."

With these words, I,_____, hanging from my cross, breathed my last human breath.

Additional scriptures for personal study:

Romans 8:3-4	1 Corinthians 1:18
Galatians 6:14	Romans 6:6
Galatians 5:24	

How is God's glory revealed through the cross?

What kinds of things do you think went through Jesus's mind as his flesh went through such a horrendous death?

He took care of your transgressions, your infirmities, your sickness—he healed you eternally. In light of his death, how do you live?

USE THIS PAGE TO JOURNAL ABOUT WHAT GOD IS REVEALING TO YOU TODAY.

JOURNAL

USE THIS PAGE TO JOURNAL ABOUT WHAT GOD IS REVEALING TO YOU TODAY.

But He was pierced because of our transgressions,
crushed because of our iniquities;
punishment for our peace was on Him,
and we are healed by His wounds.
(Isaiah 53:5)

Glory Revealed Through Prophecy

In the comedy classic *Dumb and Dumber*, Jim Carrey plays Lloyd—a fool in love who has somehow managed to end up in a conversation with the girl of his dreams, a girl that is obviously out of his league. Their conversation went something like this:

Lloyd asked, "So what are the chances of a girl like you and a guy like me... ending up together?"

"Well, that's pretty difficult to say," Mary replied

"Hit me with it! I've come a long way to see you, Mary. The least you can do is level with me. What are my chances?"

"Um, not good."

"Like, one out of a hundred, not good?"

"Lloyd, I'd say more like one out of a million."

"So Mary, what you're telling me is—there is a chance!"

To look at such odds and say, "There is a chance," is funny to say the least.

I realize that it's just a goofy movie, but there is still a point to be made. The point being there are moments when even the greatest improbabilities do have a chance to become realities.

What if I could tell you how, when, and where your best friend would one day die? What if it wasn't a typical death—but one that happens in rare cases to say the least? There are many rare causes of death out there.

For example, the chance of dying from being struck by lightning is 1 in 79,746.

Your friend could be killed by a venomous spider, but the chances of that happening would be 1 in 468,508.

God used prophecy to allow events of the past to build bridges to the future...

It's also highly unlikely that your friend will die in a forest fire—1 in 65,756. But what if someone predicted that it was going to happen? Not only that, but he told you in which forest and how old your friend would be. Oh yeah, one more thing: when his claim is made, your best bud hasn't even been born yet.

At that point, the odds would be one in tens of millions.

If it did come true, however, you would have to admit that even the greatest odds leave room for possibility.

It would definitely get your attention if the one describing an actual historical event had made the same type of predictions in the past and never been wrong. His track record would demand attention. You would wonder where he was getting his information, and his source would have your undivided attention.

The Bible shows us such people—we call them the prophets of old.

The prophet Isaiah was such a man. Along with other prophecies, Isaiah accurately prophesied, in detail, the crucifixion of Jesus Christ—some seven hundred years before his actual birth.

Mind you, I said prophesied, not predicted. There's a huge difference. Predicting means taking a guess on the basis of observation, experience, or scientific reason. Predictions come from man's reason. Isaiah's prophecy came from God-given revelation.

Through specific prophecies, God reveals himself in miraculous ways in the words of prophets such as Isaiah and Elijah.

Isaiah is the most celebrated among all of God's prophets. He had no match or rival through history. Born in Judah during a time in which there were no lines between spiritual counsel and political counsel, Isaiah thrived as a prophet under the rule four different kings. He came from a family of nobility and wealth, and his educated writings were rich with history, poetry, and prophecy.

But the role of prophet wasn't to act as some religious seer for the king. A prophet was to be God's voice for each generation, setting the stage for the divine redemption of man. God used prophecy to allow events of the past to build bridges to events of the future, glorifying God and reinforcing the character of his Word. Fulfilled prophecy got the attention of the people by revealing what no one could possibly know, and it fixed their eyes on the will of God.

Though sometimes far-reaching in time, prophets generally spoke into events that would happen within their generations. Someone in Isaiah's shoes must have known the great risk of the words of his mouth. But what must Isaiah have thought when he found himself describing in great detail the death of a Savior? Do you think he wondered whether it would be that year or ten years from then? Do you think he knew it would be more than seven hundred years in the future?

Isaiah's prophecy regarding Christ's crucifixion is simply remarkable. But take into consideration that of the almost twenty-five hundred prophecies in the Bible, two thousand have come to pass. Verbatim. And the rest are promises yet to be.

Dr. Hugh Ross, an astronomical physicist and president of the organization called *Reasons to Believe,* walks out just how improbable, and therefore remarkable, the fulfillment of some of these biblical prophecies are.

Before the horrors of crucifixion were even dreamed up, King David in the Psalms and the prophet Zechariah both wrote of the Messiah's death—describing not only the method of his death but also that his body would be pierced while his bones would remain intact. The mathematical probability of two men at different times in history getting that right is 1 in 10^{13}. That's 10 with thirteen zeros behind it!

Elijah's supernatural departure from earth being predicted by a group of prophets: 1 in 10^9.

Jeremiah predicting the exact location of Israel's nine suburbs during its second rebirth some 2,600 years ago: 1 in 10^{18}.

If you add together the probabilities of just thirteen independent and non-related prophecies being correct, the chances are 1 in 10^{138}. Written out, that's 1,000,000,000,000,000,000,000,000,000,000,000,000,000,000,00 0,000,000,000,000,000,000,000,000,000,000,000,000,000,000,00 0,000,000,000,000,000,000,000,000,000,000,000,000,000,000.

When you begin to look at just how remarkable it is that four-fifths of the Bible's prophecies have actually come true, with the remaining left for the end of days, the words take on new life. God didn't just give us a book of allegories and historical fables to glean wisdom from; he gave us an infallible treasure of the past, present, and future. The design of his Word is so perfect, we can know without any doubt that it is true.

When it comes to prophecy surrounding the Messiah, no one described it more accurately than the prophet Isaiah. Just the idea that the Messiah would come from Galilee instead of Jerusalem—which was the home of the temple and hierarchy of priests—was a controversial declaration. But Isaiah went on to say that Jesus would be rejected, inhumanely tortured, and put to death between two sinners. And all this was predicted seven hundred years before he was born.

So what if all this happened just as Isaiah said it would? How does this give me any hope today? How in the world does this apply to me and my life?

Prophecy in Scripture serves as evidence proving that the Bible is truth that withstands the test of time. It has always been accurate and will always be. When prophecies that Scripture says will happen do, in fact, happen, they help us trust that the Word of God is infallible. Thus, we can trust that God himself is infallible.

We learn to trust scriptures when we see prophecy come to fruition.

God is so gracious to remind us, over and over again through prophecy, that he is God and it's in our best interest to listen to him. It's as if he's saying to us, "I have information I want to reveal to you that will give you a future and a hope. The price? Believe in me!"

It's important to be reminded that this passage in Isaiah is one of the most controversial passages in all of Scripture. It's one thing to have a passage like this in the New Testament. It's another thing for God to have Isaiah speak it so far in advance of the coming of the Messiah.

Some scholars don't want to confess that the prophet is referring to Christ. There are synagogues that read Chapters 51 and 52 but skip 53. As much as they want to explain that this is about Israel, it's not. It's clearly about Jesus Christ.

You can't ignore God's glory revealed through prophecy here. There are a minimum of three hundred prophecies in the Old Testament alone referring to the first coming of Christ, and more than five hundred refer to his second coming. This one just happens to be the most blatant. It's the elephant in the room that no one can ignore.

Every tribe and tongue—everyone who's ever read this has had to ask themselves, "What is the probability? What are the chances?"

The French mathematician George Heron calculated that for one man to fulfill just forty of the three hundred prophecies pointing to Jesus, the odds are 1 in 10^{157}. Wow. Scriptural prophecy is not a prediction, it's a promise. It's a God-given revelation of things to come. Isaiah wasn't predicting the future; he was claiming the truth of what was actually going to happen. The prophet transcribed a love note from God to us, once again revealing God's glory.

Through prophecy, we learn to take God at his word when he reveals his plans before they happen. We also learn to trust Scriptures when we see prophecy come to fruition. We can look forward to the prophecies in his Word that haven't yet come to pass, knowing that he has yet to be wrong. But more than anything, as we trust his Word and take it more seriously, God gets glory. He's simply, undeniably showing us how in control he really is.

Additional scriptures for personal study:
Matthew 27:9-10   Zechariah 11:12-13

How is God's glory revealed through prophecy?

What is the difference between prophecy and prediction? Why is it remarkable that so many of the Bible's prophecies came to be?

How can you use the miracle of prophecy throughout the Bible to reinforce your faith? How can you use it to minister to others?

JOURNAL

USE THIS PAGE TO JOURNAL ABOUT WHAT GOD IS REVEALING TO YOU TODAY.

Now to Him who is able to protect you from stumbling and to make you stand in the presence of His glory, blameless and with great joy, to the only God our Savior, through Jesus Christ our Lord, be glory, majesty, power, and authority before all time, now, and forever.

Amen.

(Jude 1: 24-25)

Glory Revealed Through Our Inability

There is nothing certain in a man's life but that he must lose it.
—Meredith Owen

Certainty is one of the most impossible things to come by here on earth. Entire global industries are devoted to trying to figure out how to sustain wealth, relationships, and security. Even the most sought-after experts are paid to merely make educated guesses on the stock market, self-improvement, and national defense. How funny is it that the people we place our trust in are, at best, just making educated guesses?

But so few people seem to get that. Ever since September 11, 2001, the public has demanded that our government insulate us from any and every threat that may possibly surface. How many people do you think realize how impossible that is? Try standing in an airport security line more than once a week, and you'll see just how ridiculous it is to presume that the lady working the security counter can ultimately protect you from terrorism.

Don't get me wrong, these are good people, doing the best that they can, but they are only human and they make mistakes. I once accidentally got a starter pistol through security, only to realize it when I began unpacking my bag later that night. I had driven to a city earlier that week, and had used the gun for a sermon illustration. I had forgotten to take it out of my bag in order to fly home, and somehow it was never caught.

It was a sobering reminder of how most of the time we walk around airports with a false sense of security. On one hand, I have seen the airport security stop someone's grandmother from getting her nail clippers through, and on the other hand, security once let a man get on a plane with shoes full of explosives.

Let's face it. We control nothing.

This is why it doesn't say in Jude 1:24-25, "To the only airport security, that is able to keep us from falling."

The book of Jude is a short one. Just one chapter. But its message is important enough for it to stand on its own. Written by Jude, the brother of James and half-brother of Jesus, it is a letter to the church in its earliest organization. He wrote with both concern and encouragement as the first believers were struggling to reconcile exactly what it meant to be saved by Christ. His letter was essentially a warning against false teachers who were diluting the gospel and twisting God's message of grace to serve their skewed understanding. Jude's great doxology was an encouragement to the early church to keep its hope in Christ alone.

Even today, with the church and our theologies well established, we spend so much energy trying to build certainty around us that we create false bubbles of confidence made of our own strength. And bubbles they are. It doesn't take much more than a pinprick to destroy everything we work so hard to build for ourselves.

I watched a friend last year plan his annual Christian festival with an attendance expectancy of more than seventy thousand. Thousands of volunteers and millions of dollars later, it simply began to rain. The entire event had to be canceled. Year after year, the event had gone on as scheduled, but that did not guarantee that it was going to this time.

This is why it also doesn't say in Jude 1:24-25, "To the only good track record that is able to keep us from falling."

Let's face it. We control nothing. Not the weather, not wars, not the stock market—not even whether or not our loved ones will keep loving us. The pain of a broken marriage, a church split, the loss of a loved one—there are infinite levels of "sure things" from which we can fall.

That's why it's such a relief when we surrender to the fact that God is the only one who is able to keep us from falling. Not our money, not our best intentions—nothing except our Heavenly Father will keep us safe.

Jennifer and I were on a pontoon boat with her parents one afternoon when we saw a huge mansion being built on the lake. It was only halfway done, so we docked the boat and helped ourselves to a walk-through. I remember thinking to myself, *I wish I was the guy who owned this house.* The property was perfect. But all wasn't as it appeared.

My father-in-law told me the story of the family who was building the new house. The family's two-year-old had drowned in their pool with everyone just steps away from his silent cries. Every time the father caught a glimpse of their backyard, the pool reminded him of the loss of his son. The family was building a new house because the current one was haunted by memories of loss and pain. The reality is that even in the new mansion, the pain will still be there.

That is why it doesn't say in Jude 1:24-25, "To the only house which is able to keep us from falling."

You can only be dependent on a God who is stable and who has always been and who will always be. We elevate things both silly and noble into the position of God in our lives, hoping they will keep our picture for our lives intact. I can't tell you how many people go into counseling rooms shell-shocked when things they thought were in their control went awry. Or how many people lost their life savings and ended their lives after the tech crash of 2000. Or how many people living in New York will live the rest of their lives in complete fear because their sense of security was shattered on a clear September morning.

But unless we realize that God alone has the power to keep us secure, and unless we put him first, our efforts are entirely in vain.

Now this doesn't give us license to live haphazardly, making unwise decisions. You can't think, *I can do whatever I want; God's got the wheel anyway. He'll take care of me.* That's entirely backward. He's not some cosmic clean-up service. Rather, we have to put our trust in him first, living a life of obedience so that we allow him to be in all the details. If you keep in mind the eternal value of your actions, obeying him first, you'll know that whatever circumstances come your way, he ordained them.

One of the best books I've read that touches on this topic is Randy Alcorn's *The Treasure Principle*. It's actually a book about joyful giving, but it's rich with principles that illustrate the eternal value of allowing God to be first.

Randy writes of a contrast between two graves he saw while visiting Egypt. The first was one of a Yale graduate who'd used his entire inheritance to become a missionary and evangelize Muslims. The grave was simple and dusty, hidden off of a back alley—but on the epitaph it read, "Apart from faith in Christ, there is no explanation for such a life."

The other grave was so lavish that the contents were kept under high security at the Egyptian National Museum. The contents belonged to King Tut, a ruler whose treasures were buried with him for three thousand years under the premise that he could take his treasures with him to the next life.

On one hand we have the grave of a man who gave up everything he had because he knew that the kingdom of God was the only thing worth investing his treasure in. On the other, we find a museum full of priceless relics that were covered in dust for millennia while the owner faced an eternity of darkness. In the scope of eternity—whose situation was actually priceless?

There is only one true God who can keep us from falling. He is the only one who can hold all things in his hand. You can't put your security in your marriage, your children, your job, your future... you can only be dependent on a God who has always been and who always will be.

Our inability to keep ourselves from falling is the very thing that turns us to a God who is, in fact, able. It's one of the reasons Jude was warning the early church to cleave to Christ and not be distracted by the disability of man. When we are reminded that we are unable and he is able, we find ourselves free, leaning more and more on him. And through our leaning, God reveals his glorious stability.

God's ability is the backdrop of his glory.

I'll end with a quote from Martin Luther: "I have held many things in my hands and I have lost them all. But whatever I have placed in God's hands, that I still possess."

Additional scriptures for personal study:

    1 John 4:4   Isaiah 40:15

How is God's glory revealed through our inability to keep ourselves from falling?

A few times in this chapter I said, "That's why it doesn't say, "To the only _____ who can keep us from falling." Fill in that blank with at least ten different things that you struggle with trusting in place of God.

I mentioned that we elevate things both silly and noble into the position of God in our lives. What are some things, especially in the Christian culture, that we mistakenly elevate into the place of God?

USE THIS PAGE TO JOURNAL ABOUT WHAT GOD IS REVEALING TO YOU TODAY.

USE THIS PAGE TO JOURNAL ABOUT WHAT GOD IS REVEALING TO YOU TODAY.

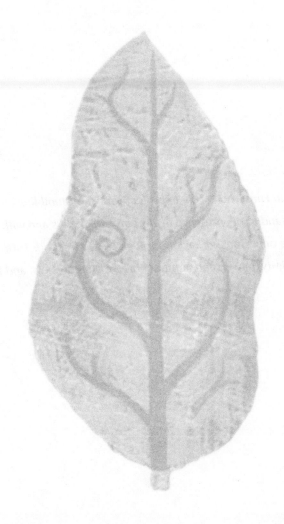

Now to Him who is able to protect you from stumbling and to make you stand in the presence of His glory, blameless and with great joy, to the only God our Savior, through Jesus Christ our Lord, be glory, majesty, power, and authority before all time, now, and forever.

Amen.

(Jude 1:24-25)

Glory Revealed Through Exclusivity

Sometimes what's meant as a compliment ends up feeling like a kick in the ribs. A few summers ago, I was speaking at a festival in California where I had the opportunity to share my testimony with a crowd of more than forty thousand attendees. At first everything seemed to go great. I remember walking off the stage after my talk thinking, *This was such a great night,* when I decided to make my way to the prayer tent to see if the counselors needed extra help with those who'd come forward for prayer and counseling.

I never made it to the tent.

On my way there, I was intercepted by a youth pastor and his wife. They had sought me out to thank me, to encourage me for meeting their group right where they were spiritually. At first I was encouraged—until they kept talking.

As it turned out, they were the leaders of a youth group from the Church of Scientology. Their aim was to include all religions in their services. Until recently, it was hard to find material that was non-offensive to everyone in their group... until one of the teens discovered modern worship music. With so many songs referring to trees, hills, skies and a nondescript God as some celestial boyfriend, they were safe!

The couple had been hesitant to bring their group to festivals fearing speakers who would offend with a "close-minded" viewpoint regarding eternity. But as they put it, I didn't offend at all. In fact, I only mentioned Jesus once or twice.

They went on and on about how refreshing it was that my message was not filled with a bunch of Jesus talk. As they thanked me, my heart sank lower and lower. The problem was not what I had *said* in my message, but what I had *not said*.

Jesus is exclusive...
there is only one God.

See, I spent a lot of energy talking about the circumstances that led me to God, but I never made it clear that Jesus Christ is the only one who could save a wretched soul like me. I didn't say that Jesus is the one who came to my rescue because he is the only one who has the power to save. I just presumed the audience got that, so I fast-forwarded through the "Christ as our only Savior" part of the gospel message. In turn, I never really presented the gospel at all.

A few hours later, I was in my hotel room on my knees praying repentantly. I made a covenant that night with God that I would never again be found guilty of not making clear the full message of the gospel. Forgetting to make known Christ's exclusivity as Savior was not common practice in my preaching, but it had been that night and I committed that it would never happen again. I had learned a valuable lesson.

Unfortunately, I am not the only one who needs to be taught that lesson. Many pulpits are filled with weekly messages like my sermon that afternoon at the festival. These pastors believe in Christ as the only way to salvation, they are just too busy addressing life circumstances to notice they are excluding the one thing that people need to hear the most.

In some instances, it is intentional. In an effort to be inclusive, a belief is taught that there are many gods and many ways to attain salvation. To many, the idea of one God and one Savior seems narrow-minded and offensive. They argue that Jesus alone sounds exclusive.

But Jesus *is* exclusive.

Not exclusive in a crude and pompous nature, but in light of the fact that the Bible makes it clear: There is only one God, and Christ is the only way to salvation. It's exclusive in that there are no other gods and there is no other savior.

Acts 4:12 says: "There is salvation in no one else, for there is no other name under heaven given to people by which we must be saved."

You and I can disagree about all kinds of things in life and agree to disagree. Who's the greatest band of all time? As a child of the 80s, I'm going to argue U2. Who knows who your favorite band is. But we're not going to hold it against each other, are we? To each his own!

Who's the greatest athlete of all time? Same story. I'm going to say Michael Jordan. You might argue Ali or Gretzky—but those aren't fighting words. That's because in the scheme of things, what music we listen to or which team jersey we wear doesn't have eternal consequences. We may get passionate about those things, but they're not so important that we'll risk everything to convince the other that our position is superior.

But bring up Jesus, and he's one of the most divisive topics in history. That's because there is power in his name.

People generally don't hate the name of Jesus; they just don't want it to be the only name. Muslims believe in Jesus. They believe that he was a good prophet. But they think that if you and I believe that Jesus is the Son of God, we've gotten the messenger mixed up with the message. Jewish people believe in Jesus. They think of him as a teacher and a rabbi. But they don't believe that he was the Son of God.

The world wants Jesus to be Dr. Phil—a feel-good, tough-love giver of good advice. They don't want him to be all-powerful. But mention John 14:6, "I am the way, the truth, and the life. No one comes to the Father except through Me," and things start getting hairy. All of a sudden, he's not just a good man—you have to choose him or you don't get to live out an eternal life.

Jude 1:24-25 says:

> *Now to Him who is able to protect you from stumbling and to make you stand in the presence of His glory, blameless and with great joy, to the only God our Savior, through Jesus Christ our Lord, be glory, majesty, power, and authority before all time, now, and forever. Amen.*

Webster's dictionary defines "only" as: 1) unquestionably the best, peerless; 2) alone in a class or category, sole.

The problem with the word "only" is that there's no way to get around its exclusivity. It takes away the conversation of "your God works for you, my God works for me—let's just move on." But plant your feet firmly on the ground declaring the sovereignty of Jesus Christ as Lord, and you'll ruffle a few feathers.

If anybody wants there to be another way, it would seem to be me. I've got an entire extended family of Muslims who are some of the most good and moral people I can point to. I would love for there to be an escape clause in Scripture somewhere. A place where there is salvation under Jesus plus good morals. But I can't help but wonder why God would send his Son if he wasn't the only way. Paul tells us in Galations 2:21, "I do not set aside the grace of God; for if righteousness comes through the law, then Christ died for nothing." If the gospel is Jesus plus good works, plus keeping the law, or plus anything, then why Jesus at all? That's a point that cannot be ignored. It's a point that God gives me ways to lovingly share with them.

The exclusivity of Christ becomes the inclusivity of the gospel.

Does this mean Muslim people are going to hell? That people who believe in God, but are members of other religions, are damned as well? I choose to look at it in a more hopeful way. My answer to that question would be that people of other religions can come to Christ—he has given us a way to salvation! You could look at it with a pessimistic view, pointing out that other religions won't get there. I'd rather say, "If you have religion in your life, you're already seeking a connection with God and I've just got to share with you the way to truly connect."

It makes the Great Commission that much more real. Suddenly, the exclusivity of Christ becomes the inclusivity of the gospel. Christ laid it out in Matthew 28:18-20 to his disciples in the Great Commission:

Then Jesus came near and said to them,
"All authority has been given to me in heaven and on earth.
Go, therefore, and make disciples of all nations,
baptizing them in the name of the Father and of the Son and

*of the Holy Spirit, teaching them to observe everything I have
commanded you. And remember, I am with you always,
to the end of the age.*

Look at the call in Romans 10:13, and it becomes even more inclusive: "For everyone who calls on the name of the Lord will be saved." This means that when I'm talking to an unbeliever, I can let them know, "There is a way—and I can't wait to show it to you!"

Somehow we're losing that in the church. We spend so much time trying to make the gospel appealing that we often camouflage what makes the gospel necessary to begin with. In doing so, we risk presenting candy-coated imitations of life-giving truth.

I've heard worship leaders with gritty voices and expensive light shows sing generic love songs that could be applied to God or your girlfriend—take your pick. I've seen pastors preach month-long series on how to make your marriage sizzle, forgetting that non-believers are in the room—people that need to hear the gospel. These things aren't bad in and of themselves, but without pairing them with the undeniable saving power of Jesus Christ, they set the stage for little more than a cultural pep rally. It's a trend that robs God of his glory.

In Jude 1:24-25, we see Jude give God glory as he celebrates Jesus in his great doxology. It's his "only" declaration that makes it so beautiful. He is saying, "You alone deserve glory, because you alone are God. You alone have the power to save. All glory to you. All glory for the only God!"

God is not interested in sharing his glory, and Jude, the author, is not interested in giving partial praise. Jude wants God's glory revealed by celebrating him exclusively.

We, too, can see the glory of God revealed by worshipping Christ as the only one who is able to keep us from falling. The only one who can present us blameless before God and give us joy.

Additional scriptures for personal study:

John 14:6	Luke 4:8
John 8:58	Colossians 1:16-17
Acts 4:11-12	

How is God's glory revealed through exclusivity?

Where is the balance between walking out the Great Commission in love and being honest with people about the exclusivity of Christ?

Take an honest look at your life. Do you leave room for anyone to doubt exactly who the only Savior is?

USE THIS PAGE TO JOURNAL ABOUT WHAT GOD IS REVEALING TO YOU TODAY.

Now to Him who is able to protect you from stumbling and to make you stand in the presence of His glory, blameless and with great joy, to the only God our Savior, through Jesus Christ our Lord, be glory, majesty, power, and authority before all time, now, and forever.

Amen.

(Jude 1:24-25)

Glory Revealed Through Power

Not long ago, a friend of mine invited me to golf's most prestigious event—the Masters. They tell me it's one of the hardest tickets in all of sports to get. Apparently, the tickets are so precious that people leave them in their wills to be passed down to their children. I wouldn't know because I wasn't much of a golf fan. Not until that day.

If you've never been, let me describe it for you. The grounds are a forest of perfection. From the perfectly manicured grass to the mammoth oak trees and serene bodies of water, with every step you find yourself completely in awe of your surroundings.

As you enter the tournament, you're handed a bulletin with information for you to read. There are biographies and stats on the golfers playing, as well as a history of the Masters. You can read up on why the green jacket is given to the winner, how Bobby Jones built the course, and so much more. It's obvious that they want you to understand you are privileged to be allowed in.

The Masters is filled with tradition. From the infamous two-dollar pimento cheese sandwiches to last-year's winner choosing the dinner menu for this year's inaugural ball, everywhere you look, there is tradition and history. Then there is the hush. The presumed etiquette demanded the moment you step on the course. You look around and notice thousands of people around you, but everyone is quiet. Golf, after all, is a civilized sport—everyone must maintain composure.

Everywhere he went, Jesus drew a crowd.

Your ticket doesn't buy you a seat, it buys you access. Many opt to stay in one place and wait to see different golfers come through. Some, however, follow their favorites from hole to hole. My friends and I opted to do a little of both. When the news got to us that Tiger Woods would be coming through, we claimed our stake on top of a hill overlooking the infamous fifteenth hole. We stayed there, waiting for over an hour, watching some of the world's best swing away. Champion after champion went by with all of their big sponsors in tow, but then we saw a real crowd.

I looked to my left and there was Tiger Woods, or rather three thousand people moving like a swarm of bees around what was rumored to be Tiger Woods. Eventually he emerged and I stood looking at the greatest player to ever pick up a golf club. Out of all of the "masters" at that tournament, he was the real Master.

For the first time that day, the hush rule was broken. Composure went out the window and with it you could feel the crowd's anticipation.

"It's Tiger, it's Tiger—he's here!"

"He looks different than on TV."

"Look at what he's wearing."

"I saw him last year, and he waved at me!"

"I can't believe we are actually going to see him swing in person!"

The swarms of people around Tiger were moving excitedly in every direction. It was a powerful tidal wave of fan mania. They did whatever it took—even climbing trash cans—to see that kind of power in action. They wanted to say that they saw modern-day majesty, authority on the green... that kind of power.

As I stood there with a bird's eye view from the top of that hill, I had an epiphany. This must have been what it felt and looked like when Jesus traveled from one place to another. This must have been the kind of frenzy the crowd worked itself into when Jesus came near. When I watched a husband put his wife on his shoulders to get a clear view of Tiger Woods, I thought of the men in the Bible who went to the extreme effort of lowering their paralyzed friend through a rooftop just so he could have access to Jesus.

Everywhere he went, Jesus drew a crowd. People packed picnics and lined roadways for the chance to hear him speak, to watch him perform miracles, to touch the hem of his garment. All this without mass emails or Ticketmaster. People came to see the Son of God firsthand. It didn't matter how long the journey or what it took to make it, they were willing to pay the price in order to see him, to experience and receive his power. They simply had to witness it first hand.

Luke 5:17-26 tells us the story of Jesus and the paralytic. Word of Jesus's miraculous power had reached a tipping point, and people had gathered from every corner of Galilee, Judea, and Jerusalem. Sure, there were people in the crowd who were there just to watch some sort of show—the Pharisees included—but there were people who needed a touch from that kind of power so desperately that they'd do almost anything to get it.

One group of men in particular were on a mission. They had a friend who was paralyzed, and they thought that perhaps this Jesus could save him from his life of misery and begging. They did their best to get their friend through the crowds, carrying him on a makeshift bed. But that plan wasn't going to work. They wanted so badly for him to have a chance at being healed that they refused to give up. Somehow, they tethered the cot, with the crippled man in it, up the roof and down to where Jesus was standing below.

The friends got Jesus's attention, but what they didn't get was what they thought they were looking for—they got something even better. Jesus commended their faith, letting them know that their sins were forgiven. Not just the cripple, but all of the men in the group. Jesus healed their eternal paralysis! After all of the great lengths they'd gone to looking for physical healing for their friend, Jesus was more interested in healing their souls.

The Pharisees, picking up on Jesus's true agenda, were enraged! No one but God had the power to forgive sin, and they had absolutely no interest in believing that this blasphemous man was the Son of God. But Jesus knew exactly what they were thinking.

Jesus said to the Pharisees, "Which is easier, to say 'Your sins are forgiven you,' or to say, 'Rise and walk?' But that you may know that the Son of Man has authority on earth to forgive sins." He then turned to the crippled man and said, "I say to you, rise, pick up your bed and go home."

Read that again. "But that you may know that the Son of Man has authority on earth to forgive sins... rise."

Jesus is basically saying, "So that you understand I have the power to save you from eternal paralysis, I'll take care of your earthly paralysis. I'm going to prove to you my glory, my majesty, my dominion, my authority as the Son of God right here and right now by healing this man. Yes I want to heal you—but what I want much more is for you to believe that I can heal your soul!"

It's obvious, when you read the story, that the men who brought their crippled friend weren't looking for salvation—they didn't even know they could get it. They just wanted a better life for their friend. But Jesus understood what the man needed better than he or his friends did. What the paralytic really needed was for his soul to be healed. God was able to use the physical need as a connection point to help him and his friends understand his spiritual need.

God might heal us physically, or he might not–that's for him to decide.

Jesus used his power to draw a crowd, to get the attention of people so they would know he was the Son of God sent to redeem them from their sins. They would see his power and believe that he could be their salvation.

But he also got to uncover his glory, his majesty, his dominion, and his authority. When his power is revealed in a tangible physical way, his glory is revealed for all to see. After he commanded the paralytic to rise, the man immediately stood, and in front of everyone gave glory to God. It stirred up the entire crowd and left them in amazement. They couldn't help but be filled with awe, saying, "We have seen extraordinary things today."

The crowds in attendance that day undoubtedly went home and told everyone they knew about what Jesus had done. They probably beat on the doors in their villages, so full of good news that they could hardly contain it. The power that Jesus demonstrated that day spilled over as his glory continued to be revealed to everyone who would hear.

You can't substitute anything in the place of genuine power. Not finely manicured lawns, not exclusive tradition... not even pimento cheese sandwiches. What draws a crowd at the Masters is seeing people do with a golf ball what we think is impossible to do. What will attract people to our faith is letting the power of Jesus show that what is impossible with men is possible with God, as it says in Luke 18:27.

God might heal us physically, or he might not—that's for him to decide. But God is still in the business of physical healing so he can say, "This is only a taste of what I offer you in eternal healing." Spiritually, we're just seeing a glimpse of his majesty and his splendor—yet physically we hope to see it because a crowd will gather, and his glory will shine.

I'll never forget the effect Tiger Woods left on the crowd as he walked away from the fifteenth hole that April afternoon. We all stood there, realizing that we had just witnessed something really special. It gave me a tiny glimpse of what it must have been like after Jesus healed the paralyzed man. In Luke's account he tells the effect on all who witnessed Jesus the Master at work: "Then everyone was astounded, and they were giving glory to God. And they were filled with awe and said, 'We have seen incredible things today!'" (Luke 5:26).

Additional scriptures for personal study:

Isaiah 43:13	Luke 4:36
Luke 4:14	Acts 1:8

How is God's glory revealed through his power?

How desperate are you for the power of God in your life?

Do you believe that God still wants to demonstrate today the kind of power Christ displayed when he walked the earth? Why or why not?

JOURNAL

USE THIS PAGE TO JOURNAL ABOUT WHAT GOD IS REVEALING TO YOU TODAY.

Now to Him who is able to protect you from stumbling and to make you stand in the presence of His glory, blameless and with great joy, to the only God our Savior, through Jesus Christ our Lord, be glory, majesty, power, and authority before all time, now, and forever.

Amen.

(Jude 1:24-25)

Glory Revealed Through Conversion

If Jude is correct about Christ being full of glory, majesty, power, and authority before all time, now, and forever, why are so many churches not filled to the brim with people? If Christ is so majestic, powerful, and glorious, then why are our Christian gatherings getting smaller?

It brings us to an interesting question: Why are people leaving our Christian churches by the masses?

In the last chapter, we talked about how genuine power draws a crowd, how people gather at any cost to see real masters in all their glory. I was reminded, on a small scale, of what it must have been like to see the crowds swarm around Jesus by seeing the crowds swarm around Tiger Woods at the Masters. The image struck me so profoundly that I began to question why we don't see that today in the church.

I left the Masters that afternoon realizing that the event is annually sold out and wait-listed, not due to manicured grass, tradition, or their famous pimento cheese sandwiches sold at the snack bar. Those things are great, but the crowds gather to watch the power of a master at work. They go to see Tiger Woods or Phil Mickelson play golf. They pay the price of a coveted ticket to have a brush with greatness—to see the power in person.

Now that golf course in Augusta, Georgia is still there after the Masters comes and goes every April. You can walk the grounds in July, go to the gift shop, eat the sandwiches, and even play the course if you know the right people—but the crowds are gone. Why? Because the masters aren't there in July. The tournament is only great because of the professionals who show up to play in it.

We desperately need the powerful presence of Jesus now.

What if Tiger Woods, Phil Mickelson, and all the other great golfers of our time decided not to attend the Masters next year? Would the crowds still be there? Maybe for the first year, but probably not the next. Some die-hards would still show up for the tradition of it, but the overall demand would likely disappear. Without the masters who make up "the Masters," that course would be no different than a typical week in July.

Let's take it one step further. What if Tiger Woods, Phil Mickelson, and all the other pros decided to gather and play a tournament at your local putt-putt course? Would it draw a crowd? The only question asked would be, *where in the world would you fit the masses of people who would pay anything to get in?* All of a sudden, the local putt-putt course, almost bankrupt due to low attendance, would become the busiest place in town. All the hype certainly wouldn't be because of the immaculate greens or even because of the faded windmill on hole number eight. It would be because of the power of the players who were showing up.

According to various statistics, church attendance is on the decline both in number and in percentages related to population growth. If present trends continue, the percentage of people who will attend church in 2050 will represent just more than 10 percent of the population.

The Barna Group reports in the year 2000, 70 percent of professed "born-again" believers expressed their faith by attending their local church. Trends predict that number will fall to 30-35 percent by the year 2025. Those are born-again believers!

There are certainly pockets of growth—churches that are growing despite the trends. But overall, people are not gravitating to church on Sunday mornings. Churches with thousands on the membership role are seeing only 40-60 percent enter their doors on a weekly basis.

Maybe it's because rather than focusing on the splendor, majesty, power, and authority of Jesus, we are focusing on the beauty of our church buildings and gadgets. Oftentimes when people attend church, what they don't see is the majestic presence and splendid power of the Master himself—Jesus.

Where's the power in our churches today that demands a crowd? Where's the resurrection power, the week-in week-out supernatural healing that draws us to church with strong anticipation? Where are the reports of droves of people drawn to church because they simply don't want to miss what God is doing in our midst? Where are the people saying, "I have to see it for myself—I have to experience it myself?"

I am not saying we need to have weekly healing services, but that we need to ask God to bring healing in our services. Sure it's happening here and there in our western culture, but broadly speaking, I wonder if we're banking on manicured lawns, tradition, and great pimento cheese sandwiches rather than on the presence of the Master. If the Masters were to stop being about the legends of the game and start being about anything else, it would eventually lose its draw. When a church service focuses on anything less than encountering the power of King Jesus, the people will eventually lose interest as well.

Never before has the church spent so much money on plasma screens, cool staging, and fine-tuning all of the bells and whistles. Cool lighting is great to have, but at the end of the day, it is just a "pimento cheese sandwich." Nothing more. If it becomes the reason to attend, eventually you'll get sick of pimento cheese sandwiches.

Don't get me wrong—the Masters is amazing because they've created an environment that does both. It honors a master golfer by giving him a great environment to display his ability. Good sound systems and great quality equipment honor God too. They show that we are about excellence for his Excellency, but it's important to make sure that it never gets out of hand. When cool staging takes precedence over the presence and power of Jesus, then we are relying on the power of a pimento cheese sandwich!

The same is true about our history and heritage as the church. Much like the Masters tournament, our history and heritage can serve as a reminder of how God has blessed in the past. But we cannot live in the past. Otherwise our church walls become just memorial tombs. We desperately need the powerful presence of Jesus now!

Christ's powerful presence is actually being experienced on a large scale in other places in the world. In China, church attendance is on a major rise. I have a friend from Iran who told me that the church is experiencing amazing growth in the Middle East. In third world countries where people desperately need Jesus, there are no places big enough for church gatherings to meet.

By and large, the church in Africa isn't packing them in due to good songs and great JumboTrons. They are seeing the power of Jesus do miraculous wonders. I went to dinner with a Jamaican friend who works for a reputable conservative ministry. I am not talking about a false prophet who claims to have powers in order to swindle people out of their money. This is a friend I have known for years. He is a true minister, filled with integrity and spiritual depth.

I listened intently as he shared with me what he had witnessed in a church meeting in Africa. He was so shaken by the power he'd seen that he was reluctant to talk to me about it. He was afraid that I wouldn't believe him. He'd seen healings—undeniable healings. He'd witnessed thousands find salvation in the name of Jesus. But the healings were more than just healings of eternal salvation—some were physical as well.

As he shared with me the supernatural healings that he'd witnessed first-hand, I sat there weeping. When was the last time we saw that on a Sunday morning in America?

Maybe it's because people in other countries are gathering to see Jesus with an urgent longing to experience his greatness. Governors will declare three-day public holidays so that all the working class people can attend crusades. Buses arrive full and leave empty. It's unusual for us to recognize the God-sized things the Lord is doing all over the world.

I contrast that against a conversation I had with a friend of mine in Houston recently. A world-renown evangelist was leading a crusade that was filled with special appearances by some of the biggest names in Christian music . The event was free to the public, and the goal was to invite non-believers to come and hear the gospel through great preaching and worship. I asked my friend if he was planning to attend, but he wasn't sure. Downtown parking was always a hassle.

Parking was a hassle? Tell that to the guy in Africa who walked for two days just to be one of a million people standing in the heat waiting to experience the hope, conversion, and healing that only Jesus can offer!

Have you ever noticed how, in the Bible, Jesus allowed signs and wonders to reveal his power to people. Christ used physical conversion to parallel the more important eternal conversion. It's interesting to me that Jesus's first conversion was turning water into wine. I find this fascinating for a few reasons. First, that he chose a physical conversion as his first miracle. He knew that physical evidence demanded attention. Jesus was revealing his power with a physical conversion for our physical eyes to see. Talk about evidence that demands a verdict and draws a crowd! How many invitations to weddings do you think he got after that? It was a bold statement.

The second fact I find fascinating is that Jesus chose to turn water into wine. Why didn't he turn wine into water? It still would have been a miracle. No one else could have done it. Could it be that he took something common and turned it into something infinitely more interesting? Wine has texture. Wine is strong. Wine is intoxicating. Wine evolves and gets better with time. Wine is alive.

Christ used physical conversion to parallel the more important eternal conversion.

Jesus took a dead Lazarus and made him alive. He could have taken living people and supernaturally stricken them dead. That certainly would have commanded attention. But that's not what he did. He could have saved Lazarus's soul without resurrecting his physical body. But Jesus brought Lazarus back to life. He used physical healing to draw a crowd and verify that he is the Son of God.

Jesus is a powerful God. He brought attention and glory everywhere he went. He made dead people alive; he didn't make alive people dead. He healed the blind man's eyes; he wasn't looking to blind men. He took something as bland as water and turned it into something as potent as wine. And Christ did all this to prove that he could save people's souls. It seems to me that these days the American church is content to turn water into sparkling cider.

When we allow the conversion power of Jesus to work in our lives, we become the "water turned wine" to everyone around us. We become living wine that grows so strong over time that people can't deny the eternal healing that's taken place in our lives. They yearn for the same—opening the door for the power of Christ to work in their lives too.

Now granted, there's a strand of Christianity that may have tainted the water for the rest of us. There are highly publicized ministries out there that claim supernatural power and miracles. But somehow, instead of the glory going to God, it goes to other things. But that doesn't mean that the rest of us should steer clear from the power that the name of Jesus holds. People need the real power of Christ!

You've heard the saying, "If it sounds too good to be true, it more than likely is." There are so many things out there claiming to be powerful. Between the amount of junk email in our in-boxes and a television crammed with one too many infomercials, we're conditioned to view anything that claims to have power as suspect. It's one thing to be cautious and careful, it's another to be fearful and jaded.

Pray with me that God begins to soften our hearts to allow his powerful presence back into all of our churches. I know he is everywhere at all times, but our prayer can be that he shows himself in such a powerful way that more and more people will be drawn to the one true God. Let's pray that empty pews will be filled with those who desire to experience the converting power of Jesus. Not for our sakes, but for his glory to be revealed!

Additional scriptures for personal study:
  Psalm 115:17-18   Colossians 2:13-14
  Romans 8:10-11   Mark 6:7

How is God's glory revealed through conversion?

What would compel a lost person to come to your church on a Sunday morning?

Would you know what to say to someone who trusted God for healing and didn't get it? How would you answer their hard questions?

USE THIS PAGE TO JOURNAL ABOUT WHAT GOD IS REVEALING TO YOU TODAY.

USE THIS PAGE TO JOURNAL ABOUT WHAT GOD IS REVEALING TO YOU TODAY.

A voice of one crying out:
Prepare the way of the LORD in the wilderness;
make a straight highway for our God in the desert.

Every valley will be lifted up,
and every mountain and hill will be leveled;
the uneven ground will become smooth,
and the rough places a plain.

And the glory of the LORD will appear,
and all humanity will see [it] together,
for the mouth of the LORD has spoken.

(Isaiah 40:3-5)

Glory Revealed Through Arrows

If you ever see Billy Graham on the street, be sure to go up to him and let him know that you just finished reading my book. He'll probably hesitate for a moment and then pretend he doesn't know me... but that's our thing. We're actually great friends. I walk him through delicate political matters when he's dealing with heads of state, and he helps me write my sermons. We're fishing buddies, and our wives swap secret recipes.

I hope you know I'm kidding. The truth is I've had the honor to work with the Billy Graham Evangelistic Association a number of times in different capacities. But I've only met Dr. Graham once—at a Billy and Franklin Graham crusade in Albuquerque, New Mexico. I was there to speak at a pre-crusade rally and give my testimony on the youth night. Of course, I wanted to know if I was going to get to meet the man who's preached the gospel to more people than anyone in the history of this planet.

One afternoon during the four-day crusade, I was invited by the crusade coordinator to go to a luncheon with twenty or so dignitaries. It was going to be a time of honoring Dr. Graham. I was thrilled, even though they let me know that I probably wouldn't get a chance for a personal greeting. I was actually in good company. The governor, some congressmen, and many other luminaries were in attendance, yet no one had the opportunity to say a word to the aging evangelist. Due to time constraints and ill health, Dr. Graham only had the capacity to greet the waiters, the cooks, and the chef—graciously thanking each one of them for their hard work. I thought that gesture was amazing, but I have to admit I was still pretty disappointed.

It wasn't until the stadium event a few nights later that I had my brush with greatness. Sitting on the platform after giving my testimony, I noticed a figure being wheeled up the ramp to the stage. I was totally awestruck. There he was—still such a giant long after his physical strength had departed. His body was obviously weaker, but his message was still as powerful as it ever was—maybe even more so because of the contrast.

Needless to say, I was entirely taken aback when one of his handlers wheeled him toward me and made an introduction.

"Dr. Graham, this is David Nasser, a young evangelist."

Those words took on so much meaning in light of who they were uttered to.

"Dr. Graham," I managed. "I'm speechless."

It was so amazing to be in the presence of a man who has defined modern-day evangelism. Here was one of the greatest living arrows to ever point people toward Christ, and I had nothing to say.

Much like Dr. Graham, John the Baptist was an evangelist. He was put on earth to let everyone know that Jesus was no false alarm—the Savior was coming, just as Isaiah the prophet foretold. In fact, John did such a great job that the Bible actually goes on to point out that he wasn't the light—just a big arrow pointing to the light (John 1:6-7).

Jesus himself said in Luke 7:28, "I tell you, among those born of women no one is greater than John, but the least in the kingdom of God is greater than he."

Talk about an endorsement! What preacher wouldn't kill for that kind of sound byte? But that wasn't the point. Jesus was basically saying, "The reason John is such a great man is because he has not only figured out, but also carried out, his very reason for existence in life—to ultimately point people to me. He is great because he understands why he exists. You can be great if you understand why you are made as well."

A great piece of art deserves a beautiful frame—but not one so outlandish that it competes for attention. A frame just gives the artwork context—the art is the whole reason the frame exists! Would you be more likely to spend a whole day in a frame shop or in an art museum?

In the music world, a truly great producer is worth their weight in gold, but you don't buy tickets to go see a producer in concert. You go to see the artist! That's because the job of the producer is to take the artist's message and help them express it as clearly as they can—to masterfully frame the artist's work.

Are you getting in the way of pointing others to Christ?

It's always a fine line in the studio to keep the production—the arrangement, the effects, the bells and whistles—from getting in the way of the song. A great producer knows exactly how to dance around that line by only bringing in the pieces that perfectly accent the artist's emotion. They phrase the breakaway melodies and instrumentation in such a way that frames the very heart of what the artist is trying to convey.

The best producer gets out of the way so that the artist can shine. He does his job with excellence and stays the course—he doesn't under-produce or over-produce. If he's doing his job, you'll never even notice his name in the credits—you'll just tell everyone you know to pick up a copy of the artist's fantastic new album.

You never want the frame to outdo the art. And you never want the producer to take over the music. John the Baptist, though proclaimed great by Jesus himself, was great only because he served as a frame to the greater message. He didn't skew the story of the coming Messiah to fit his own elaborate agenda or purpose. If you remember your Bible stories, he ended up headless. His whole reason for existing was to relay, at any cost, "Hey, get ready. The real deal is coming!"

John 3:30 says, "He must increase, but I must decrease." Said another way, "He must become greater, I must become less important." John the Baptist is saying that he's just an arrow pointing to God the Father.

Let's take this one step further. Philippians 2:7 says, "Instead He (Jesus) emptied Himself by assuming the form of a slave, taking on the likeness of men... He had come as a man in His external form." If Jesus as a man thought it important enough to give up his reputation to lead us to God... how much more should we? Jesus as full man humbled himself to show us Jesus as full God.

Ask yourself this: Are you getting in the way of pointing people to Christ? Are the motivations behind what you do for God truly revealing him? Are you continually pointing to his glory?

Sometimes in trying to seek God, we get so distracted looking at the arrows that we stop looking at what they're pointing to. We get so caught up in the messenger that we miss the message.

It's one thing to love your pastor, it's another to set him up as a mock savior. Show me a church that falls apart at the seams when the pastor steps down or leaves for another calling, and I'll show you a church caught up in the pastor. Pastors exist to help us worship God. They don't exist to be worshipped. They are voices crying out in the wilderness saying, "Prepare the way of the Lord. He is coming!"

We're of greatest use to God's kingdom when we reshape our lives to direct all attention to him.

I, too, fight this. Many times, I find myself feeling indebted to certain ministers. I have to work hard not to idolize some writers and pastors just because I've received so much through their ministry. It's one thing for me to say, "Man, you're a great mentor." But I have to be careful to draw a thick line to make sure I'm not worshipping them.

When I was that young evangelist sitting on the platform behind Billy Graham, I basked in the glory of our encounter. It was like I'd been given a golden ticket. I met Billy Graham. Sure it was only for a few seconds, but who cares—Billy Graham met me! Mesmerized by my brush with greatness, I rewound the moment over and over again in my head while I watched him speak.

I totally missed the point... until Dr. Graham finished his sermon and gave the altar call. Dr. Graham asked those who desired to receive Christ as Savior to come to the altar for prayer. People from all over the coliseum began to come down to the front. They were coming not to meet Billy Graham—they were coming to receive Christ.

As it turned out, thousands of people met Jesus that night. I just met Billy Graham, his faithful messenger. I couldn't get past the idea that I had met such a spiritual icon while his desire was to introduce people to Jesus. He was the arrow, pointing the way, but I was so caught up in the street sign that I missed the grand spectacle. I almost missed out on the glory of God, substituting it instead with the glory of Billy Graham.

On a personal note, I can tell you that I sound a lot more spiritual in this book and in my sermons than I really am. It's not that I'm a fake, it's just that I'm not God. I write and talk about the Lord as one of the many voices he uses to point people to him. Sometimes, on a very, very rare occasion, a person might get hung up on the voice instead of the message coming through me. But if I'm being faithful to use the natural voice God has given me to shout in the wilderness, he will still get the glory.

God has given you a voice as well. Maybe you're loud like a bullhorn, reverberating in people's souls. Maybe your voice feels more like a whisper, gentle and reassuring. The truth is that God reveals himself through different voices. We just need to make sure that we use the voice he has given us to point to him.

Some of us are called to be flashing neon arrows, reflecting his light. Others of us may be called to be subtle, gentle guides, quietly leading the eyes of those around us upwards. Whichever our calling, we're of greatest use to his kingdom when we reshape our lives to direct all attention from ourselves to God and his glory.

Could you be turning legitimate arrows into idols? Recently I was in New York City for what was supposed to be the final Billy Graham crusade ever. I saw a lot of people who were there only to catch a glimpse of the great evangelist before God took him home. They went to see an icon before he died. However, God was still drawing people to himself even in the midst of their clamoring to encounter the messenger. Hundreds, even thousands, ended up coming to a saving knowledge of Christ. Many went so they could say they saw a man before he died, but they ended up encountering a God who gave them life.

Dr. Graham is an arrow, just like the rest of us are called to be. And when we use the natural voice that God gives us to direct people to him, we effectively frame the masterpiece that is his message.

Call Billy Graham what you want. A legend. A frame. A bullhorn. An arrow. Or simply a voice.

Just don't call him the Way. That name is reserved for only one. His name is Jesus.

Additional scriptures for personal study:

2 Corinthians 2:14	2 Corinthians 4:7
Jude 1:25	2 Corinthians 12:9

How is God's glory revealed through arrows?

Who are the biggest arrows pointing to God in your life? What qualities do they have that can help you redirect your heart and your mind toward Christ?

Is there anything in your life preventing you from being a shiny, reflective arrow of God's glory? Your attitude? Your insecurity? Your pride? Your disobedience?

USE THIS PAGE TO JOURNAL ABOUT WHAT GOD IS REVEALING TO YOU TODAY.

A voice of one crying out:
Prepare the way of the LORD in the wilderness;
make a straight highway for our God in the desert.

Every valley will be lifted up,
and every mountain and hill will be leveled;
the uneven ground will become smooth,
and the rough places a plain.

And the glory of the LORD will appear,
and all humanity will see [it] together,
for the mouth of the LORD has spoken.
(Isaiah 40:3-5)

Glory Revealed Through Preparation

Red carpets gather a crowd. Think about all of the madness that accompanies a "red carpet event." Flashbulbs. Cameras. Outlandish fashion. Celebrities. Dignitaries. Heads of State. Reporters. Gossip columnists.

But you can't have a true red carpet event without a crowd—every person clamoring to catch a glimpse of someone important. The bigger the buzz, the bigger the crowd. The bigger the crowd, the bigger the celebrity. But it all starts with the rolling out of a carpet and the setup of a velvet rope. And those symbols are enough to make a crowd start to gather.

In ancient times, whenever a monarch was traveling through conquered lands, returning home from battle, pioneers were sent ahead to make a wide path through rough territory. The ruler wanted to set up a prime opportunity for everyone to witness and celebrate the great homecoming. The pioneers would level mountain passes, making the roads clear and wide. They were literally preparing the way—removing anything that would interfere with the pomp and circumstance of the imminent royal arrival. Their objective was simple—create a corridor worthy of a king and his armies so that the people could see them parade in all of their glory. It was the earliest version of rolling out the red carpet.

I can imagine bystanders asking, "What are you doing? Why all the fuss? What's so special about this road to put so much effort into it?"

The pioneers would respond, "It's not the road we're preparing. It's the way for the triumphant king."

That's an important distinction. People don't generally gather to admire a red carpet. Their excitement has nothing to do with the velvet pile or how dramatically long it is. It's all about the anticipation of who might be coming through.

One day on our honeymoon in London, Jennifer and I were on our way to a museum in Trafalgar Square when we heard a phrase that stopped us in our tracks.

"The Queen is coming!"

Those words were enough to halt our plans for the afternoon. Sure enough, we looked around, and we were in the middle of an event of royal proportions. We watched, fascinated as the barricades were put in place and people abuzz with anticipation began to line the streets. Guards were assembling and street sweepers were making final preparations. As the crowd grew, it was clear that the royal coming was imminent.

When the parade finally began, we'd been waiting for so long that Jennifer and I had made ourselves comfortable sitting on the ground. That changed when I looked up from the cobblestone to meet the stern gaze of a British man, eyeballing me as if to say, "Don't you know better than to sit in the presence of the Queen?" We stood up immediately—we got it.

And then came the majesty. First were the gallant horses trotting with their heads held upright in attention. Marching just behind them were the soldiers of the Royal Guard in a formation so perfect, you almost wanted to toss something at them to see if they were human. But all of this was merely a setup heralding Prince Charles riding his horse, leading the Queen and the rest of the royal family through their people. That moment commanded attention from everyone—even from those of us for whom the British crown had no authority.

Looking back, we didn't wake up that morning and think, *I wonder if there's a parade? Maybe the Queen of England will be out for a stroll!* It hadn't even crossed our minds when we planned our honeymoon whether or not we'd see the Queen. What trumped our plans for the day was merely the sound of a voice. We gave up our entire agenda for a glimpse of royalty.

I wonder what kind of voice would cause a non-believer to stick around for a glimpse of Jesus? What kind of statement would compel someone with their own agenda to lay it aside and clamor for a glimpse of God passing through?

We're preparing the way for Jesus.

It's the church's responsibility to roll out the red carpet for Jesus on the earth. To be a voice that causes people to stop and notice. To sweep the landscape of our hearts and our culture so that people will begin to anticipate something so great that a crowd naturally assembles. To get people to stop and ask, "Why are you doing what you're doing?" So that when they see us stand up, they can't help but do the same.

We're preparing the way for Jesus. When we live our lives as arrows pointing to him, we are preparing the way for Christ to be known to others. In John 1:23, John the Baptist is saying, "I am a road builder. I am not the way, but I am a voice." He was rolling out the red carpet so that everyone would begin to expect the arrival of Jesus.

But preparing the way isn't just for the benefit of the onlookers. It also shows our adoration for the One who made the way for us.

Whenever you are honoring the arrival of special guests, you don't just do the ordinary, do you? You pull out all the stops. You set aside a date and time and send out invitations. You put balloons or candles at the entrances, maybe arrange fresh flowers where there are usually none. You put out your best food and drink for everyone to enjoy. Through your actions, you let everyone in attendance know just how special the guests of honor are.

Not long ago, we threw a huge party for all of our friends. It's not something we get to do very often, so we were determined to make it special. Jennifer handled most of the niceties, but I took on the most glamorous job. I re-leveled our gravel road. My son Rudy, a bunch of guys, and I spent a weekend with a few metal rakes and a truckload of gravel.

Was the road passable before? Sure it was. But that wasn't the point. I wanted our guests to spend the evening feeling honored. I wanted to set the stage for the great time ahead. I didn't want them the least bit distracted as they came or went. I just wanted them to remember the fun they had—to drive away knowing they are loved by our family.

If I'm willing to go to these lengths for my friends, shouldn't I be taking extra care preparing the way for Christ in my life? Ephesians 5:27 tells us to, "present the church to Himself in splendor, without spot or wrinkle or any such thing, but holy and blameless." I need to spend every day of my life refining and aligning my life, honoring his place in it so that others are drawn to his grand procession.

I told you earlier about our real-life encounter with British royalty. It was a great example to get us to the point I am trying to make, but like all illustrations, it has its limits. British royalty is influential in England's affairs, but in all actuality, they have no real power. The days of British monarchy are long gone—what remains is a royal family that has an influential voice in Britain's politics, but doesn't have final say. This is where the illustration begins to separate itself from Jesus as sovereign King.

Jesus is our true King and he holds all the power over heaven and earth. His arrival into our lives is in no way symbolic—he sets aside all phonies and redeems us from all sin. Christ will be the great equalizer. While red carpets and barricades are meant to separate us from the royal procession, Jesus came so that we could go to the Father directly. And when Jesus returns to earth, there won't be barricades. We'll get to join him in the great procession for the rest of eternity.

But the biggest difference is this: When Jennifer and I left the royal parade and went on about our honeymoon itinerary, the excitement quickly wore off. To be quite honest, I wondered if our time would have been better spent in the museum rather than watching a bunch of men with fuzzy hats prance around a tin-can throne.

When Jesus enters the scene, it's never disappointing. In fact, we look for ways to change our agenda to help further prepare the way for him. We can do this practically by something as simple as putting time into a Sunday school lesson. We can memorize scripture. Or we could study up on other cultures so that when an opportunity arrives to build relationships, we can roll out the red carpet for Jesus to show up in our everyday lives.

But we're also preparing for his return. We honor him by carrying out the Great Commission with urgency, knowing that he could come at any time. We tell others that he's coming back as we wait by the ropes, longing for his return. When the crowd gathers around the road that we've so carefully prepared, no one who's ever been touched by the passing of the glory of God will say, "Is this all I got?"

Additional scriptures for personal study:

Jude 1:25	2 Corinthians 5:18-19
Romans 1:16	1 Thessalonians 1:5

How is God's glory revealed through preparation?

What are the gravel driveways in your life that could use some leveling to honor Christ? Where are the places where you're "sitting on the ground" instead of standing up to honor God?

What are some ways that you can lay out the red carpet in your community? How can you help gather a crowd for the sake of the gospel?

USE THIS PAGE TO JOURNAL ABOUT WHAT GOD IS REVEALING TO YOU TODAY.

JOURNAL

USE THIS PAGE TO JOURNAL ABOUT WHAT GOD IS REVEALING TO YOU TODAY.

In 1979, radical Muslim zealots overthrew the Iranian government in a revolution that took over one million lives. David, only nine at the time, and his family were forced to escape, finding refuge in the United States. At eighteen David, through the graceful witness of a youth group, became a Christian.

Today David speaks to over seven hundred thousand people annually, using relevant, inventive methods to connect to a post-modern generation. And as the author of *A Call to Die* and *A Call to Grace*, David has sold well over 100,000 copies in a few short years.

David and his family, Jennifer, Rudy, Grace, Pearl and Sarah (the cats), Mr. Bubbles (the goose), and Curly (the duck) live in Birmingham, Alabama.

Glory Revealed, the Word of God in Worship is a ten song, Scripture-driven worship project. The songs on this CD are the passages inspired from *Glory Revealed,* the book.

Featuring ALL NEW Recordings by:
Trevor Morgan, Third Day's Mac Powell, Steven Curtis Chapman, Brian Littrell, Hyper Static Union's Shawn Lewis, David Crowder, Shane & Shane, Candi Pearson-Shelton, Josh Bates, Michael W. Smith, Starfield's Tim Neufeld, and Casting Crown's Mark Hall.

Contact D. Nasser Outreach at 205-982-9996 for more information or visit www.davidnasser.com.

A 39 day look at how
the grace-filled life is
not about doing but
about being.

A book/journal
focusing on what it
means to live for Christ
by daily dying to self.
For 40 days, the reader
will fast from the world
to feast on God.

Contact D. Nasser Outreach at 205-982-9996 for more
information or visit www.davidnasser.com.

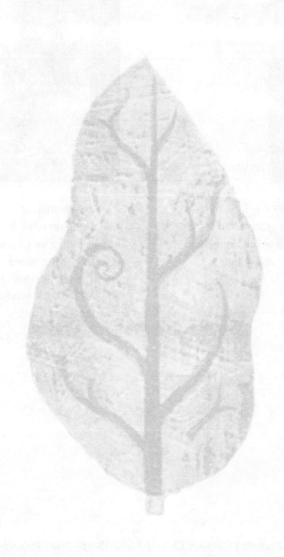